SACRED
Darkness

Other Books by Paul Coutinho, SJ

How Big Is Your God?

Just as You Are

An Ignatian Pathway

SACRED
Darkness

ENCOUNTERING DIVINE LOVE IN LIFE'S
DARKEST PLACES

PAUL COUTINHO, SJ

LOYOLA PRESS.
A JESUIT MINISTRY
Chicago

LOYOLA PRESS.
A JESUIT MINISTRY

3441 N. Ashland Avenue
Chicago, Illinois 60657
(800) 621-1008
www.loyolapress.com

Art credit: © Ricardo De Mattos/Getty Images

Library of Congress Cataloging-in-Publication Data

Coutinho, Paul.
  Sacred darkness: encountering divine love in life's darkest places / Paul Coutinho.
      p. cm.
  ISBN-13: 978-0-8294-3353-1
  ISBN-10: 0-8294-3353-8
1. Spirituality. 2. Wilderness (Theology) 3. Light--Religious aspects. 4.
Light--Religious aspects--Christianity. 5. Light and darkness in the Bible. 6.
Spiritual life. 7. Spiritual life--Christianity. I. Title.
  BL624.C693 2012
  242--dc23

                                                            2011045387

Printed in the United States of America.

12 13 14 15 16 17 Bang 10 9 8 7 6 5 4 3 2

Dedication

To the Eternal Spirit dwelling at the core of our being
and all those whose wisdom and support I experienced
in the dark recesses of life.

Contents

PART ONE
Universal Darkness

Human beings naturally long for light and try to escape the dark. In fact, we tend to equate darkness with evil. Yet the spiritual wise ones among us have always understood that at the core of our humanness—and in our very divine origins—a fathomless darkness abides and does its necessary work. In darkness we meet the quiet and holy; in darkness we encounter God in a way that is unnamed, formless, and beyond ordinary comprehension. At the heart of the human experience is beauty that is immense, mysterious, and universal.

In the Beginning . . .

Life begins in darkness and ends in darkness. In the beginning, there was only darkness. According to the Bible and according to science, it is from this darkness, emptiness, and nothingness that all of creation comes into being. Darkness is a mystery; it evokes curiosity and fear of the unknown, and at the same time it brings us into the embrace of reality. This reality is all around us, pregnant with the existential truths of life.

That darkness at the heart of creation has its counterpart in the darkness living at the core of each of us.

As the sacred story states, "The earth was empty and without form and darkness covered the face of the deep." Out of this darkness God commanded the revelation of light. This light was not the sun or the moon but light that came *from within the darkness*. This light is an integral and essential part of the darkness. That darkness at the heart of creation has its counterpart in the darkness living at the core of each of us.

In the dark moments and struggles of our lives, we often realize the beauty and the power that lie deep within us. This darkness sheds light on our external world and helps us not only cope with, but also live effectively and more fully in, the painful situations of our lives. This light comes from the darkness at our core. This light—the light within the dark cave of our being—draws us back to the very source of life. There is comfort, there is peace, and there is power in the dark cave of our being where God truly dwells.

Darkness and the Purer Vision

In darkness we experience pure life. What we see in external light is colored by our prejudice or whatever mental framework we have developed. If we are not careful, we will see life, not as it is, but as *we* are. Reality as we know it is often shaped by our experiences, our family values, our religion, our culture, and many other human factors.

But in darkness we relate to people as persons without being influenced by their gender, race, culture, or religion. In darkness we experience a connectedness with everyone. We find this to be true, for example, in times of personal, communal, and natural disasters. In times of illness we will accept blood from people of any race, religion, or culture. We will accept the best doctors and look beyond the color of their skin, their religion, or their sexual orientation. A few years ago, the electricity in St. Louis failed for a few days. During this time of darkness it was amazing how, for the first time, neighbors got acquainted as persons and reached out to others as humans. We now attached names to people we had known only by the dogs they had walked down our street every day. Soon people planned neighborhood celebrations. Floods, drought, hurricanes, and typhoons often have the same effect: they humanize people and build a global village.

There is an Indian story about a holy man who sat at the entrance of a cave and promised that anyone who entered the cave would see God face-to-face. Crowds rushed to the cave, only to learn the important condition to this promise: those who wanted to see God face-to-face had to have their eyes plucked out before they entered the cave.

In darkness we experience God as God without making God in our own image and likeness. In darkness, specific religions lose their monopoly over God. Dogmatism and interreligious wars become redundant or irrelevant. With our many-colored filters removed, the human spirit launches on the quest for the one true God. Darkness actually purifies our vision—some of our anthropomorphic images of God slowly fade away. Then we can begin to experience God as God.

Darkness, Word, and *OM*

We may discover God as Logos, the Word. One of the Hebrew understandings of Logos is energy charged with power. This energy was in the beginning with God; this energy *was* God (John 1:1). This is the energy that hovered over the primordial darkness and brought forth a new and beautiful creation by pouring the divine essence into all of creation. This is the same divine energy that God breathes into you and me, making us human, giving us identity as the divine breath (Genesis 2).

One of the Eastern creation stories is similar to the Bible story. "In the beginning was the only Lord of the Universe, His Word was with Him. This Word was His second. He contemplated. He said, 'I will deliver this Word so that she will produce and bring into being all this world'" (*Tandya Maha Brahmana*, 20.14.2). In the beginning, the world was a vast dark ocean that washed upon the shores of nothingness. From the depths of the dark waters the sound of *OM* (pronounced aum) began to find its way through the waters and filled the emptiness of the world with throbbing energy. This creative energy, like the Logos, was without beginning or end. *OM* was with God and was God.

OM is the symbol of the Absolute, the omnipotent, the omnipresent, and the source of all existence. *OM* is the life energy that runs through our very breath and pervades all life. It is the one eternal syllable that is more than a word; it is an intonation. It is the basic sound of the world and contains all other sounds. When it is intoned, it is like music that transcends the barriers of age, race, culture, even species. If repeated with the correct intonation, it will resonate throughout the body so that the sound penetrates to the person's core. This simple but profoundly sacred sound generates harmony, peace, and bliss. It projects the mind beyond the mundane world and at the same time makes the Absolute more tangible and understandable. When we chant *OM* we create within ourselves a vibration that is attuned with the cosmic vibration. The momentary silence between each chant becomes palpable. The mind moves between the reality of sound and silence until the sound fades *into* silence. In this silence there is no thought; it's a state in which the mind and the intellect are transcended as the individual self comes together with the infinite self.

The deeper we delve into the subconscious and unconscious, the darker and more real life gets.

Think of the human person as three levels of being: the conscious, the subconscious, and the core that is our unconscious. The conscious or the surface level is always in flux and expends a lot of energy. The deeper we delve into the subconscious and unconscious, the darker and more real life gets. At this deepest, darkest level we find the stability—and liveliness—of Logos and *OM*. That sacred energy of life flows from the darkest depths within us to continuously create new life. We can think of it like this: we breathe in energy from the universe, and it becomes a life force as it goes through the dark recesses within us. When we breathe out, there's a little death that creates space for something new.

4 Darkness as the Source of Life

The beginning stages of life are fragile, and darkness has the amazing power to nourish this new life. Human life begins in the darkness and intimacy of the womb. In that sanctuary, new life is nurtured. It grows, and divine breath takes root in the clay body of the baby (see Genesis 2). Eventually the baby is strong enough to enter the light of the outside world—even though, in the end, that body will die and return to the darkness of the earth.

Like humans, all other living things, as well as other elements of creation, are nourished and strengthened in darkness until they are ready for the light. In the mystery of darkness, divine energy is poured into every creature, and the whole of creation thus becomes the temple of divine presence and essence (cf. SpEx 39).

The splendor of the mighty oak develops from a seed planted in the earth's darkness. Each flower, regardless of size, is able to penetrate through the dark earth and grow delicate and beautiful! The butterfly forms in the darkness of the cocoon until, now a beautiful winged creature, it breaks into the light. And the most precious elements and minerals are all carefully hidden and protected in the womb of the earth; even the pearl is formed in the darkness of an oyster shell.

Until humans harnessed electricity, we had little control over the darkness, and we developed reverence for the sacredness of the dark. Darkness conceals everything outside and draws us within and beyond ourselves. The life energy that is spent in the daylight is rejuvenated in the night. At the end of the day we pass from the activity into the darkness of sleep and are revitalized.

The Jewish Sabbath and other feast days begin in the evening as the sun sets. The Hebrews began each new day with the sunset; thus the day begins with darkness and Jewish communal life begins there. The Hebrews seemed to understand that darkness is the ground of being. A person won't get to the depth of him- or herself until that person is at home in the dark. Dark places are like transit places. If we use transit times properly, we will find new vigor and energy for the next stage of our journey.

5 Death and Darkness

In many ways death seems to be the darkest moment of our lives. We tend to feel quite helpless in the face of death and dying.

William Shakespeare marveled at how humans feared death, which he believed would come at the appointed time for each person. Our fear of death will not prevent it from happening. Neither will it allow us to live fully. That is why Shakespeare would famously proclaim, "Cowards die many times before their deaths; The valiant never taste of death but once" (*Julius Caesar*, Act 2, scene 2).

There is a story of the man who came down with a rare illness. The doctors had given him three years to live. After struggling with this reality and coming to terms with his imminent death, the man began to live his life as he never had before. He first went through all his material belongings, taking the time to appreciate the significance of his possessions and the people connected with each of them. Then, with much gratitude, he gave them away one by one.

He reflected on his life and forgave himself for all his faults and failings; he reconciled himself with those who had hurt him or treated him unjustly. He admitted his own guilt but did not torment himself over his past. He lived his life with much patience, understanding, and compassion. Little, if anything, would upset him now—anger, hurt, jealousy. He lived his life free, full, and happy.

But after a year had gone by, the doctors called him with much excitement. They called him to their office to give him the good news that a cure had been found for his otherwise terminal illness. When the man heard this, to the amazement of the doctors, he broke down and cried bitterly, with much sadness and distress. He wondered if he could continue to live this happy and free life—or would he soon revert to his old ways, now that he was given apparently unlimited time?

As Jesuit novices, on the first Sunday of every month, we had the "Preparation for Death" devotion. We imagined our death: the people around our dead body, the things they were saying, our funeral with all its details. We dwelt especially on the way people would summarize the meaning and message of our lives. By facing the reality of death, we were inspired to live our lives as fully as we could—and in the way we wanted to be remembered. We got into the habit of thinking that every day could be our last day to live. When we felt this reality in our gut, we cherished every moment of that day and gave it our very best.

God whose divine breath gave us life will with that same breath sustain us as we live for all eternity.

In fact, death is the final and most sure doorway to life. When someone is dying, we help them in the process by working on the surface disturbance and inconsonance. We help them stop fighting death and continue to journey with life. We release the grip on those transitory illusions of life: material possessions, work, titles, even the people who have been gifts loaned to us on life's journey. We come to a realization about the essence of life—namely, that God whose divine breath gave us life will with that same breath sustain us as we live for all eternity.

When we watch a loved one die, perhaps we shed many tears. But sometimes through those tears we see a rainbow we didn't expect. The treasure at the end of the rainbow—the treasure we find in darkness—is the understanding that death is the end of physical life, but it's not the end of relationship.

There is another story of a baseball fan who was visited by an angel. The angel shared with him many things about God and life after death. The man listened carefully and then sheepishly asked the angel if there was baseball in heaven. Heaven would not be complete without baseball for this enthusiastic sports fan. The angel began to describe the great fields and the exciting baseball games that they played in heaven. And in the same animated tone, the angel announced to the fan that it was his turn to pitch the next day.

If it were your turn to pitch tomorrow, would you be ready?

6 The Darkness in Which We Worship the Divine

In various sacred writings, God's dwelling place is often referred to as the holy of holies. This is a most inviolable and private place, and its atmosphere is quiet and peaceful. This *sanctum sanctorum* is often darker than the other areas in the worship space. In Judaism, this is the innermost shrine of the tabernacle and the temple.

The *sanctum sanctorum,* or the holy of holies, is typified most effectively in traditional Hindu temples. Most temples will have a sacred symbol sculpted in black stone at the entrance of the temple to designate the presence of a sacred or divine place. Outside the temple there is often a square cistern in which devotees who have traveled from faraway places can purify their bodies, minds, and hearts before entering the temple. This water is always flowing to keep it clean and to remind people that if we desire purity, then we need to be moving constantly in our spiritual life and our relationship with God. Pilgrims and devotees then enter the temple barefoot as a symbol that they keep the impurities of the world outside and also as a sign that they empty themselves and open up to receive the divine presence. As they move toward the innermost part of the temple, they pass through candles and incense and the many images of God, and the light fades incrementally until they enter the *garbha gudi,* which is the "Cosmic Womb." In the darkness of this *sanctum sanctorum,* the devotees experience the deepest intimacy with the Divine. They have the *darshan* of God, which is an experience of seeing God and being seen by God. It's easy to see the similarities between this Hindu experience and the Christian Easter, in which divine presence is associated with the dark yet transformative emptiness of a tomb.

The Muslim mosque, or *masjid,* is a place for prostration or bowing before the Divine. As Muslim devotees approach a mosque, they are greeted with minarets and domes. The call for prayer goes out from the minaret, the highest point of the mosque. The minaret points skyward and reminds those who enter the mosque to raise their hearts and minds to God. There are ablution facilities outside for the purpose of ritual cleansing. After washing, the worshippers are prepared to allow God to come to them in every way possible. They enter the prayer hall barefoot and ready to bow several times to empty their hearts, minds, and souls so that God may fill every part of their being.

The bright lights from the outside world fade slowly as people move into the prayer hall. The prayer halls are often bare so that worshippers' focus is on God and God alone. For this reason men and women pray separately in the mosque. The focus in the prayer hall is the *mihrab,* a wall niche that indicates the *qibla* (direction) that points toward the sacred *Kaaba*, a black cube in Mecca, Saudi Arabia, that is the central point of Islam. During the *hajj,* or the holy pilgrimage to Mecca, Muslims go around the *Kaaba* seven times. Through the darkness of this black cube, Muslims experience both inner cleansing and union with the Divine. The Quran states that when Muslims pray five times a day wherever they are, they turn their faces in the direction of the sacred *Kaaba*. This brings about union of hearts among the believers, and if they truly believe in God and let God guide them, then all the divine favors will be poured into each of them. All Muslims, therefore, face the *Kaaba* when they pray. This symbolically forms the Muslims into a well-knit community in which everyone is equal in prayer. Muslims also bury their dead with their heads in the direction of the *qibla* that points to the sacred *Kaaba*.

It seems rather paradoxical to think of God's dwelling place as total darkness. In sacred texts as well as various religious teachings, God is often portrayed as light. Yet the sacred darkness—of Jewish temple, Christian church, Hindu temple, Buddhist temple, or Muslim mosque—became symbolic of God's dwelling place.

7 God of the Israelites Dwelt in Darkness

There are many references in the Bible that do surprise us with the reality of divine darkness. We are told that God comes down during the day as a thick dark cloud and speaks to Moses in the presence of all the people (Exodus 19:16–19). In the darkness of the thick cloud, the fears and insecurities of Moses melt away; the worldly voices that might draw him or distract him cannot penetrate this cloud. When our lives are shrouded in darkness, like Moses, the only voice we will hear is the voice of God. The only message that we will pass on is the one we receive from God.

At other times God soared on the wings of the wind and dwelt in a canopy of darkness (2 Samuel 22:10–12; Psalm 18:11). When the wind turns into a canopy of darkness, it becomes most powerful. This is an invitation to soar on the wings of the wind and get rid of baggage: our material clutter together with our psychological and emotional experiences, both positive and negative, and our worldly and religious doctrines and philosophies. Then we can fly free and high on the wings of the Spirit and let that Spirit alone be our guiding principle and force. This is how we can live in that canopy of darkness where God dwells.

The darkness itself draws us into a personal union and intimacy with the divine presence.

Solomon also declared that God would dwell in darkness (1 Kings 8:12; 2 Chronicles 6:1). It is in the darkest situations that we can more easily experience the wisdom to discern between the eternal and the transient aspects of life.

God made a covenant with Abraham in the darkness of the night. God was present to the people as a pillar of fire in the midst of the night. In this darkness, God cannot be identified by any gender, color, or race. In this darkness God is not somewhere "up there" and far away. The darkness itself draws us into a personal union and intimacy with the divine presence. The pillar of fire burns away all the differences created by race, gender, or color; the fire destroys all illusions and theologies. We are left with an ineffable experience. We experience that presence most intimately deep within our very being.

When God made a covenant with the people of Israel, Moses was drawn into the thick darkness where God dwelt (Exodus 20:21). It was in this experience that the people of Israel would hear God saying, "I shall be your God and you shall be my people." This covenant was the same one God had made with Abraham, and it included all the families of the earth (Genesis 12:3). It is in the darkness of this thick cloud that every human person will experience divine intimacy.

Treasures in Darkness

I stumbled upon one fascinating passage that speaks of God offering treasures of darkness that are stored in secret places (Isaiah 45:3). These gifts are universal and are given freely to anyone who knows how to receive them. God offers the treasures of darkness to a pagan king, Cyrus, to prove the authenticity of the gift and to enable Cyrus to experience the real divine presence.

When we are in pain, darkness seems to overshadow us. But often life's darkest moments offer the most precious gifts. Pain is a reality in everyone's life. How we handle this pain will either make us or break us.

There is a story of a man who was shipwrecked and found himself on a lonely island. He built himself a little house on a treetop, where he would be safe from any wild animals. He kept all his little belongings and the tools of his livelihood in the safety of his tree house. That place was his haven; there he found personal safety and could look out in hope for the ship that would one day rescue him. His home became his shrine—it was where he felt the closeness of his God.

But one day he returned to his tree house to find it in flames. All his securities were burnt to ashes. While the man sat brokenhearted and wondered about his life and his relationship with God, he looked across the waters and saw a ship on the horizon. Soon a motorboat made its way to the island. Before he knew it, the man was aboard the ship, on his way to a new life. When he asked the captain of the ship how he knew there was someone on the island, the captain told him that he had simply responded to the fire signal.

This story made me reflect on my life and on life itself. I reflected on the times when God sometimes burns down all our securities so that we can discover divine treasures in those dark moments. Through those experiences we begin to live life more fully, with greater freedom and deep inner peace. Most of us have stored away painful experiences, hiding them in places others will never enter. In time we, ourselves, tend to forget these experiences. But they continue to influence the way we live. The buried pain affects our relationships with people—and in a very real way it attracts more negative experiences. We race through life with our brakes fully on.

But when someone we love gently and lovingly burns down the fortification of those dark vaults and we begin to take a fresh look at the experiences hidden there, we will begin to find a new way of living. We find not only our personal freedom but also a burst of energy. This personal transformation sometimes sends us into the world as catalysts for change.

I am thinking of the many victims of injustice, those who have been physically, mentally, and emotionally abused. There are the millions who suffer because of unjust social and political structures. The human spirit is waiting to be free and burst forth from the rubble of injustice. People are waiting for a prophet, a guru, or a sage to dive into their darkness and release their power and dignity.

My heart goes out especially to certain women I have encountered who were sexually abused as children. Because of the abuse, unhealthy emotional patterns developed. Out of this pain, some abuse survivors became good at pretending they were fine, even the life of the party. The unhealthy craving for attention and love affected all their relationships, especially those with the people most significant to them: husband, children, family, and friends. These damaged patterns of emotion and behavior sometimes attracted more abuse; other times the survivors themselves drew people close, only to withdraw later or inflict other pain. Those women who had the courage to recognize the source of this pattern were able to free themselves to live a new and thriving life. Not only this, but these very women have also gone out to share their stories and experiences with young women in colleges and with parents of primary-school children. The results have been phenomenal. The treasures these women found in the darkest recesses of their lives helped them live in greater fullness and become authentic champions in freeing other people.

These women never forget the pain of their unjust situation, but now they live the fullness of life in love and compassion. They respond to the injustices in the world rather than react to them. They look for solutions rather than focus on who is to blame. They seek reconciliation rather than punishment. The experience of these liberated women can be the experience of anyone who is a victim in any situation. The human spirit is capable of infinite possibilities; the human spirit is capable of *divine* possibilities.

Divine treasures are hidden in the depths of darkness. This darkness might be memory, sickness, old age, or broken relationships. One of the means to bring out these hidden treasures is pain. When we are in pain, we often lose control of the situation, are thrown into chaos, and grope in the dark to find our foothold. This darkness can either make us or break us. We know that pain is a fact of life. We also realize that pain we don't resist purifies and enlightens us, but pain we resist becomes suffering. Suffering and misery, then, are a choice we make.

9 Fading to Silence, Becoming Children

When the light fades and darkness envelops our world, that darkness brings with it a profound silence. In that silence, the exterior objective world fades away, inviting us to look at the inner darkness, where we begin to experience true reality. We have no choice but to look inside ourselves to find an inner light. The images and experiences of the past come alive; we see people, places, and things that were significant. And the importance of these experiences becomes more and more clear. We hear voices of those whose words sank into our very souls. Some of these experiences were good, and some were not so good or even harmful. We look at them for what they are and let them go without making judgments about them. And we begin to experience peace in the depth of inner silence and darkness.

We know it is not wise to hold on to negative experiences and the harmful influence they could continue to have on us. We might believe that we need to get rid of the negative experiences and hold on to the positive ones. But the positive experiences are equally crippling. They may have given us glimpses into the essence of life, but if we cling to those incomplete revelations, they can become obstacles to our seeing the fuller picture of life.

Sometimes it's helpful to talk about our negative and positive experiences several times over so that we normalize them in our thinking. This will help us come to terms with these experiences. By facing them we overcome the temptation to avoid the pain of the negative experiences or to boast about the positive ones. We thus integrate these experiences and live with greater peace and freedom. The noise of our constant mental narration will slowly sink into the depths of silence.

Everything we have ever learned has perhaps helped us live more effectively. But all learning is partial truth, and as long as we grasp our learning—even our religious learning—too tightly, we will not be able to experience what Jesus called abundant life. In our psychological and spiritual darkness, religious truths and dogmas fade into oblivion, and the essence of life emerges. The noisy theological arguments fade into the insight of mystical silence.

There's the story of the two-year-old who was eager to spend time alone with her newborn sibling. The parents allowed her to do this, although they listened at the door. They heard her say to the baby, "Please tell me what God looks like. I'm beginning to forget."

This story has been told in different variations, but the message remains constant: as babies and small children we understood the mysteries of life and of God. We had a natural connection to the very essence of life. But as we grew up, we were given words and labels that took away the mystery and the hidden meaning of life. We learned concepts that destroyed the fuller significance of things. As human culture educated us, we lost the mystery and the reality of darkness, silence, and the depth of ourselves as marvelous creatures loved by our eternal God.

A child discovers a little bird and is fascinated. She wakes up every morning to watch the bird and is so thrilled and happy. Then one day the mother teaches the child that the bird is called a robin. While the mother and the other adults are excited that the child is learning new words, the child begins to lose the mystery and the charm of the robin.

This child stops experiencing the mystery and magic of this robin. The child now identifies an object that it calls a robin.

A child does not make distinctions about a person's appearance or race or beliefs. A child responds like the sun that shines on everyone and the rain that falls where it wills without discriminating between categories of persons. But as the child grows, his perception is colored by what he learns from others; thus, he begins to react differently to people and situations. In the uncluttered landscape of a child's world, there is only bliss. This is why we will never enter the kingdom of God unless we, too, become like little children.

10 The Sacred Power of Darkness

B uddhists have a saying: If you see the Buddha, kill him. The Buddha wanted us to be lamps unto ourselves. He wanted us to fall back on our own personal experience of God and of life and to take responsibility for our actions and our beliefs. He wanted us to go into the depths and darkness of our being and find our own enlightenment.

Buddhists attain enlightenment through a variety of ways. The goals of Buddhist meditation are insight and tranquility. One way of achieving insight and tranquility is to observe words, ideas, images, and thoughts that come up within us and let them pass without reflecting on them or passing judgment. The aim is to empty the mind completely. In the silence and darkness of this emptiness, we experience insight into true reality.

The other way of attaining enlightenment is through the awareness of body sensations. This awareness helps us find the interconnectedness of mind and body. The awareness of body sensations helps those memories that are embedded in the body to dissolve and allows the life energy to flow more freely within the person. This brings about a balanced mind full of love and compassion. Then we realize the unity that exists in all of life.

There is a group of Buddhists who make a retreat that they call the Darkness Retreat. They go into a dark cave and spend extended time there. The length of their stay depends on age, education, and ability—some stay for years. The preparation for this retreat is very rigorous. The spiritual guide will make sure that the one desiring to make this retreat is able to feel content and balanced during long periods of stillness.

While retreatants are in this darkness, they sit alone and become more and more aware of themselves. Their life experiences begin to surface in the form of sounds, lights, and rays that rise from the depth of their subconscious or their deep unconsciousness. In the darkness of the cave, they have no expectation of light from the outside and so begin to look for the light that comes from within their hearts and their spirits.

Their life stories unfold in the form of visions. These visions can be negative—full of lust or dread and causing anxiety and fear. But some visions are pure, full of what is good and beautiful. Often the image of the Buddha will appear along with many of the spiritual experiences of the past. Persons spending such intensive time in the cave are taught to look at all these thoughts, feelings, and visions without judging them or trying to get rid of the negative ones or cling to the good ones. When these experiences are observed and not reflected upon or judged, they simply flow out of their system, negative and positive alike. The visions are a sure sign of inner changes. These visions rise from the depth of their subconscious or their deep unconsciousness, but they are also linked to the eternal divine life.

It is possible to create this life-giving darkness without retreating into a cave for months, or weeks, or even days. We can try it out for a short period of time. Find a familiar place in your home that can be as dark as possible. Now enter that room with your eyes open. If you close your eyes, your mind will spontaneously create mental images. Darkness is neither good nor bad. Darkness just is. As you stare into the darkness, your eyes might begin to fill with tears or feel irritated. But as the real darkness begins to enter you,

you will experience profound soothing. This darkness empties everything that is negative within us, and eventually the source and energy of life flows in us with no obstacles. All fear is consumed by the darkness, and the only experience we have is love.

If we sit in prayerful silence, we can learn to observe our thoughts, feelings, and memories, and let them go.

We don't need to become Buddhists or find a dark cave in order to experience such inner purging and healing. For centuries, people of all faiths have entered darkness through silence and solitude. If we sit in prayerful silence, we can learn to observe our thoughts, feelings, and memories, and let them go. As we learn to remain still and nonjudgmental, we can experience God's embrace and understand that we are indeed partaking of the divine nature and are one with God. For those of us with deep or traumatic wounds, it is wise to seek a spiritual director or someone trained in deep meditation to guide us in this transforming prayer—just as those following practices such as the Darkness Retreat have been accompanied by guides and gurus.

The core of our being is dark, and silence pervades our innermost depths. Here everything disappears except profound and sustained peace. Our thoughts and feelings, our joys and sorrows, and all our fears melt away in the darkness. We lose all feelings of individuality and separation from the rest of creation. We cease to be an island but more like an ocean, vast and eternal. We experience ourselves as eternally united with God. We become who we are meant to be.

Be Still and Know That I Am God 11

B*e still . . .*"
    "Be still" is one of the most effective means to become peaceful and concentrated, to attain knowledge, and to experience God. We know this phrase from Psalm 46, but the concept of stillness permeates traditions other than Christianity. In the Eastern tradition stillness is described in different ways. *Samatha* or *tatasthabhava* denotes sameness or equality. It also means equanimity or perfection. The Bhagavad Gita describes the significance of stillness and its effects through many verses. The person who strives after stillness begins to feel hatred for no earthly being; is friendly and compassionate; does away with any selfish thoughts of "me or mine"; is the same in pleasure as in pain; and has a single purpose of attaining or realizing God (BG 12:13–20).

Stillness creates self-assured persons who are not elated by insight and enlightenment nor horrified by delusions. There is equanimity when faced with clods of earth or stones or gold; the wise, the friendly, and the enemy do not have any personal affect, nor does praise or blame. The secret is not to take any of these personally while they are committed in loyalty and love to become conformed to the Divine (BG 14:22–26).

Those who live by their immortal spirit have renounced the fruit of their actions. They experience serenity as they walk in the freedom of total detachment. As the waters flow into the sea, fulfilled, whose ground remains unmoved, so, too, do all desires flow into the heart of a person. And such a person wins peace. Such a person is never perplexed but even at the time of death lives with the assurance of being absorbed in the divine stillness (BG 2:69–72).

Finally, the *Gita* exhorts a seeker to sit, the self all stilled . . . integrated yet intent on the Divine. Thus the athlete of the spirit is constant in integrating self with the mind restrained; then will that peace dawn that has final liberation as its end and that subsists on the Divine (BG 6:14–15).

The Buddhists talk of stillness as mindfulness. A mindful person lives not as the *me* but as the *I*—the *I* that is the breath of God, spiritual and divine. When a person lives fully in the here and now, he or she experiences eternity. This present moment is part of every moment from the beginning of time, and until the end of time. Therefore, this present moment is eternal. Similarly, this place is part of everywhere and a part of the whole of creation from the beginning of time until the end. Mindful living is divine living.

". . . and know . . ."

Knowledge in the Eastern tradition is that which touches the heart and changes our lives. To know is to acquire wisdom and understanding. It is *vipassana*, insight or looking deeply. The Buddhists believe that when we touch the source of our true wisdom, we touch the Divine in ourselves and in every person we meet. In fact, we reverence the sacred in every part of creation.

Knowledge in the East is also as an experience of *advaita*, nondualism. Other human beings and I are not one, but we are not two; we are not one with creation, but we are not two; and God and I are not one but neither are we two. There is an interconnectedness with the whole of creation and with the divine essence. Therefore, whatever happens to one individual affects every other human being and the whole of creation. St. Paul echoes this in his letter to the Romans: "For creation waits with eager longing for the revealing of the sons of God . . . because the creation itself will be set free from its bondage to decay and obtain the glorious liberty of the children of God. We know that the whole creation has been groaning in travail together until now; and not only the creation, but we ourselves, who have the first fruits of the Spirit, groan inwardly as we wait for the realization as sons, the redemption of our bodies" (Romans 8:19–23).

Stillness and mindfulness have proved to be the most effective way of attaining that knowledge of the Divine that touches our hearts and transforms us into our true spiritual—divine—nature.

When the Buddha was questioned about the secret of his mystical pathway he said, "We sit, we walk, and we eat." Everyone does this, and yet there is no enlightenment. "When we sit, we *know* we are sitting. When we walk, we *know* we are walking. When we eat, we *know* we are eating."

This mindful living gives insight to the nature of reality and liberates a person from suffering and confusion. A person lives on a deeper plane and thus heals inner wounds through love and understanding. The greatest present we can give to anyone is to be truly present and mindful.

The experience of "no-thingness" is an outcome of mindfulness. When we experience our no-thingness, we become everything. Like Mary in her Magnificat, we too can exclaim, "The Lord has looked on the no-thingness of his servant. From henceforth all generations will call me Blessed!" This is true knowledge. It gives us our identity as spiritual and divine beings. This is also the knowledge of no-thingness that St. Paul attained through his mystical experience: In God there is neither Jew nor Gentile, male or female, slave or free (Galatians 3:28).

Sunyata is another way the Buddhists would express no-thingness. This cannot easily be expressed in words but is realized through personal experience. The Buddha experienced *sunyata* as emptiness, realizing that all things are in a state of flux. It is therefore difficult to be attached and to cling to things that are not permanent. The result is a freedom that one experiences with no more suffering even in the midst of all the pains of this life.

Sunyata also brings one to the concept of the "no-self," the *anatta*, in Buddhism. It is the invitation to realize that the ego is an illusion and causes all personal suffering. An egoless self will help one live by the true self that is both spiritual and divine. St. Paul reflects this reality when he exclaims, "It is no longer I who live but Christ who lives in me!"

"I am God!"

We have seen that both stillness and knowledge bring us to the realization of our true identity, which is deeply spiritual and divine. With the great Teilhard de Chardin, we come to realize that we are spiritual beings having a human experience rather than human beings looking for spiritual experience. We realize our biblical identity as God's image and likeness. We recognize also that it is God's breath that gives life to our ever-changing and perishable bodies. And, finally, we understand, as did the first Christians, that it is in God that we live and move and have our being.

Stillness and St. Ignatius

12

B e still and know that I am God" is so very Ignatian. St. Ignatius of Loyola wanted followers of his pathway to excel in the qualities of what the Buddhists call *samatha* and *tatasthabhava*. In the Principle and Foundation of the Spiritual Exercises, Ignatius wants us to be indifferent to health and sickness, wealth and poverty, honor and dishonor, a long life or a short one. Ignatius will insist we need to focus on being co-mingled with the Divine (SpEx 23).

Ignatius instructs that the spiritual director or companion must stand by, acting more like the pointer of a scale that helps the other person perceive equilibrium, or lack of it. We are to allow the Creator to deal directly with the creature and the creature with its Creator and Lord. The result is that the Creator will draw the person into an embrace that will melt in the Divine (SpEx 15).

Through the additional directives he gives in the Exercises, Ignatius fosters stillness and mindfulness (SpEx 73–90). He begins by helping us take care of the two most important moments of our day: just before we go to sleep and when we first awaken. These are the moments when we fall into the darkness of sleep and wake up from the wisdom and reality of that same darkness. Ignatius encourages us to decide what time we will awaken. He wants us to get clarity as to why we want to wake up and then to stay focused on the meaning and message of our lives as we prepare for our prayer (SpEx 73–74).

Just before we begin our prayer or activity, Ignatius's stillness and mindfulness become *acatamiento*, reverence. This attitude of reverence culminates in the deepest intimacy and co-mingling with the Divine, "like the rays of the sun and the sun, the waters of the fountain and the fountain" (SpEx 237). This Ignatian divine communion is like salt dissolving in water.

In the scheme of the Spiritual Exercises, Ignatius has offered five Exercises every day. Each of these prayer Exercises initiates deeper stillness and mindfulness until it culminates in the prayer of the Application of the Senses. This final prayer can be compared with a person in the presence

of the striking cobra. There is total stillness and mindfulness, and the whole experience is a mystical one. This is an
egoless state of *anatta*. The Application of the Senses draws
out the spiritual and the divine identity of the one who is
making this prayer.

> **[Ignatius] insists that we live every moment as if it were our first, last, and only moment.**

Ignatius wants the Application
of the Senses to become a way of
life, and so he also insists that we
live every moment as if it were our
first, last, and only moment. He
wants us to pray as if there were no
expectation of any fruit outside this prayer (SpEx 11). He
wants us to give ourselves to our task as if it were for this
that we were born. He will tell those in training that studies
"in a certain way require the whole person" (Const. 340)
and so does everything that we are called to do. Stillness and
mindfulness are the doorsteps to divine union and
communion.

Other helps that Ignatius offers to create stillness and
mindfulness are body posture (SpEx 76), the power of
thinking (SpEx 78), the use of light and darkness (SpEx 79),
control of the senses (SpEx 81), and penance (SpEx 82–90).
Purity of intention is a tool that Ignatius gives us to attain

anatta, egoless self. Abnegation and mortification help us live the fullness of life without the selfish ego.

Experience for Ignatius was the school of knowledge. In his autobiography Ignatius makes a very bold statement when he says: "If there were no Scriptures to teach us these matters of faith, he would be resolved to die for them, solely because of what he had experienced" (AB 29). Soon after this, Ignatius goes on to share the experience of his Great Illumination: ". . . the eyes of his understanding began to be opened; not that he saw any vision, but he understood and learnt many things, both spiritual matters and matters of faith and matters of this world and with so great an enlightenment that everything seemed new to him" (AB 30).

In his Journal entry of February 19, 1544, Ignatius is narrating all the deep insights he has received about the divine mysteries: ". . . very many lights and spiritual memories concerning the Most Holy Trinity which served as a great illumination to my mind, so much so that I thought I could never learn so much by hard study, and later, as I examined the matter more closely, I felt and understood, I thought, more than if I had studied all my life." *Sunyata* cannot be explained with the head or felt in the heart, but it is grasped by the spirit who expresses it with sighs too deep for words (Romans 8:26)!

Ignatius has thus attained wisdom and understanding through *vipassana,* insight that touches the source of true wisdom. Ignatius experiences the Divine within himself and that overflows into each person he meets and into all of creation. Everything is gift. God dwells in these gifts as if it were his temple and his own image and likeness. God labors in these gifts to perfect the temple and the image and likeness of God. The gift finally bursts forth with its spiritual and divine identity (SpEx 230–237).

Part Two
Personal Darkness

It is wise to acquaint ourselves with the characteristics of universal darkness. However, each of us eventually needs to face darkness at a very personal level. Obviously I cannot explore your personal darkness or anyone else's; all I have is my own story and the stories of people close to me. I trust that, as I delve into my personal story, its details will ring true somehow in your own experience.

The Powerful Experience of Darkness in the Retreat

13

An Indian story tells of a holy man who sat at the entrance of a cave and promised anyone who entered the cave that they would see God face-to-face. Crowds rushed to the cave only to have the holy man instruct them to pluck out their eyes before they entered the cave.

This story reminds me of Jesus' warning that we not try to get the speck out of another person's eye until we have removed the log from our own. In order to see God face-to-face, we first have to get rid of the log that blinds us. It is the log of ignorance. Or it is the log of doctrine, theology, and philosophy that has formed a filter through which we view everything. We have to pluck out our eyes—our way of seeing—so that we can experience God and life with freshness and clarity.

I once gave a retreat to a group at the end of a three-month Ignatian seminar. We were at the Jesuit retreat house in Goa, India, that overlooked the Arabian Sea. The retreatants pondered on how big they could imagine their personal God. Most of the group fell back on some favorite Scripture passage that helped them express their image and experience of God. One particular retreatant could not get into the prayer and felt very discouraged. He began by looking at the basic catechism that had introduced him to God and kept his faith alive for many years. He then went through his Jesuit training and especially the years he had spent studying philosophy and theology. He even searched through the many retreats he had made in the past. All seemed like a futile exercise. He went through the same experience that Ignatius had; he was making the retreat just as he had done all his life as a Jesuit. Ignatius writes clearly from the very beginning that the Spiritual Exercises are not done or made but are received.

Later that day, when everything was dark, he turned away from the noise and glitter of the summer beach. He was drawn in a deep and an inexplicable way to the vastness, and as the darkness covered the face of the deep, he broke down and cried uncontrollably. He had finally found what his soul was thirsting for. He experienced the immensity of his personal God. Ten years later that experience still remains fresh and continues to sustain, nourish, and deepen his relationship with God.

The great expectations of this young and eager Jesuit to get into prayer and experience the Divine failed that day, which led to discouragement and the overshadowing of the darkness in his innermost self. But then as he surrendered to the darkness that covered the face of the earth, suddenly there was a spark in his soul, opening his eyes to the Infinite Divine in a very real way.

14 Seeing God Face-to-Face

I remember well my own ordination retreat. For fifteen years I had studied the Spiritual Exercises of St. Ignatius. I had taught several courses on the spirituality of St. Ignatius and had even given these Spiritual Exercises to others in some form or another. I always knew it was vitally important to prepare for the retreat experience—to have a disposition of openness to God and an availability to God's action in my prayers. I had, therefore, gone into that retreat fully prepared and well disposed. I wanted it to be the best preparation for this new life I was about to embark upon—my life as a priest. I wanted to be the best instrument in God's hands and the most effective channel of God's graces for all to whom I would minister.

On the first day, my retreat director asked about my prayer and how I was doing. I told him that there was nothing special to report but that I was okay. This was just the first day, and I was certain the gifts I was seeking would soon appear. I was confident that God would reward my sincere openness and generosity. I was receptive to the action of God and made myself available for anything God wanted to do. I wanted God's gifts, not for my own gratification but so I would be an effective instrument in working for the divine kingdom. I stilled my body, mind, and heart, using every exercise of awareness and breathing I knew. I slowed down my pace outside of prayer and made no eye contact with anyone because I wanted to be with God alone every minute of the day. I emptied my mind of all thoughts except those that reflected my relationship with God. My heart was alert to any sign of the presence of God when I was awake and when I was asleep. I was more and more open to my retreat director and listened very attentively to everything that he said. In prayer I felt like a bullfrog sitting very still, waiting for an insect to happen by.

And nothing happened. Every day my prayer experience seemed drier than the day before and void of any tangible experience. Every day my director would ask the same set of questions, then instruct me to carry on. At our meeting on the sixth morning, I told my director that I had prayed for him—I had prayed that God would put some sense into his silly head. Every day I was telling him that I had no experience of encountering God, and all he had to say was "Carry on!"

But then a most surprising thing happened—God complained of exhaustion from trying to reach out to me.

That night when I went to the chapel to pray at my usual time, I felt so alone and in some ways quite discouraged. My favorite Scripture passages did not move me; the prayer method I had used for many years did not work. The only prayers I'd been able to make during the entire retreat were "Lord, I believe; help my unbelief" or "Lord, I believe; strengthen my faith"; and my favorite and constant prayer: "My soul is thirsting for you; when shall I see you face-to-face? My soul is thirsting for you; I want to see you face-to-face."

On that sixth evening, night's darkness filled the chapel, and around 1:00 in the morning I had a vision of myself on an island. The ocean's waters began to rise up and isolate the island from the mainland, and all of a sudden God appeared on that island, and I was face-to-face with God. I was so ecstatic and at the same time so worn-out and broken that I wanted to rest in God's lap. But then a most surprising thing happened—God complained of exhaustion from trying to reach out to me—and I found God's head resting in my lap. At that moment I broke down and wept uncontrollably.

In the darkness of that night and the emptiness and void in my soul, I had a face-to-face experience of God. People may call it a vision, a hallucination, or anything else. The details do not matter. All I know is that the experience was so real that I have never been the same again. God became the seeker, and I was the one sought (Psalm 139).

15 Seeing God's Face Is an Invitation to Die

After my ordination retreat experience, I returned to my community. I had invited a group of four men to join me living in the slums while we went through our studies in theology. The reason for living among the poor was to root our theological studies and insights in real life.

The first six months of our theological reflection seemed good because we had a priest as our guide. But he sensed fundamental problems and decided to return to the larger Jesuit community. We had no leader now, and each of us went his own way. The poor in the slums challenged us to live authentic lives, but the same group of people could draw us into their lifestyles. My companions accepted some of the attitudes and values of the people we were trying to serve; subsequently, two of them became addicted to alcohol. Socializing among these folks took the place of any serious study and theological reflections or conversations. Prayer and the Eucharist did not exist for our group.

As I began to reflect seriously on the value of our group experiment, I sent a note to the superior of the Jesuit theology and philosophy students with a list of concerns for which I sought help and clarity. The superior read the concerns as allegations, which he took personally, and from then on all hell broke loose for me. I left the small group and joined the larger community of about 200 members. The superior called me almost weekly to tell me that if there was one person he did not want in his community, it was me. He accused me of being self-righteous and not a group player. He managed to turn some of the faculty and many of my fellow companions against me. And when it came to approving me for ordination, he fasted for three days to find out what St. Ignatius would do with a person like me. He wrote a very scathing report about me but finally gave permission for my ordination. The Bombay superior who was responsible for us looked into the matter and postponed the ordination of one of my companions by three years and gave his permission with some reservations for the ordination of the other. This other companion died within a year after ordination.

During this year of turmoil and persecution, I felt completely alone. The only one who knew my inner struggles and pain was my spiritual director. Every day I felt as if I were being drawn deeper into an inner darkness. And through my painful and lonely tears, the only thing I could hold on to was the rainbow of hope and strength I found in my retreat experience. In a very strange and paradoxical way, there could not have been a better preparation for my life as a priest. In the darkness of this experience I was more grounded in my relationship with God, and the power of the Divine flowed easily through my weakness.

I have seen this pattern in the lives of those I directed in retreats and to whom I offered spiritual direction. Every time they had a profound experience of God, they soon faced darkness and unprecedented trials in their personal lives—and came out the better for it. Their life stories remind me of Abraham, who became a blessing as he passed through the darkness of the desert and the challenge of being asked to sacrifice his only son.

Power in Weakness   16

Ten days after my ordination to the priesthood, I gave my first eight-day Ignatian retreat to a group of nuns. They were older and more experienced than I was; they were leaders in their province: sisters in charge of the formation of other sisters, principals of schools, and superiors of their local communities. Each of them had been in the religious life for many years.

Not surprisingly, they felt that they had a schoolboy giving them a retreat, and one of them took it upon herself to say so. The little confidence I had mustered evaporated with these comments. I sweated all through the first talk I gave them that night. I concluded by saying that I knew that they could manage their retreat on their own and that they were free to come to me—or not—for spiritual direction during the retreat. I did share with them that St. Ignatius gave a lot of importance to having a spiritual director during the retreat process. I had a sign-up sheet; all twenty-two sisters came to see me, on alternate days.

In the darkness of her struggle with an immovable rock, God's power was made perfect in her life and her ministry.

Of course, I was nervous about directing the retreat, but I also knew that I could count on God's working through my weakness. That's exactly what happened. With every talk, I gained confidence in sharing my insights about the Spiritual Exercises. In every interview with individual sisters, I could see the wisdom and the power of the Spirit working. And I was given another grace I will never forget: I learned that the fruits of ministry are not mine. My job is to be a channel so that God can work through me and touch hearts and change the lives of people to whom I minister. After that retreat experience, I felt so light—I was free of a great burden, one I had carried many years. I realized that I was not responsible for the outcome of the retreat. It was not my job to change anyone.

One sister broke down and cried during one of her interviews. She was dealing with what had been a major problem for her for many years. She referred to it as a huge rock in her life; after all her efforts, the most she could do was chip off a bit of that rock. In my innocence I told her to leave the rock alone but rather plant a rock garden. The garden would represent her gifts and talents and all the good she had experienced. The rock, of course, was there to stay, and thanks to that rock, her life would have character. In the darkness of her struggle with an immovable rock, God's power was made perfect in her life and her ministry.

Another sister had leadership responsibilities for twelve years both in her ministry and among the sisters. She told me on her first day how she always looked forward to her annual retreats. She had a personal ritual when she first entered her retreat room. She would invite Jesus to come and live with her in that room for the eight days of her retreat. She said confidently that her Jesus never failed her. But at this retreat she could not find her Jesus. Her prayer was dry and her God very distant. This was the first retreat I had directed, and I was not sure how to handle this experience. I asked her to see me every day, and every day she told me the same thing. I fell back on my own ordination retreat. I felt sure that God was very close to her, but I could not convince her. She cried in her sadness and discouragement. Her retreats were so important to her, and her relationship with Jesus sustained her during her busy days the rest of the year. She put her trust in my confidence that everything was okay and that Jesus was in fact very close to her. And then on the sixth day she came and told me that Jesus had come to her while she was asleep. She opened her eyes and saw the physical body of Jesus by her bedside. She experienced deep satisfaction and went back to sleep. When she awoke, her prayer was still dry, but she maintained a deep sense of Jesus' presence.

Soon after the retreat this sister was elected to be in charge of all the sisters of the Bombay Province. This new ministry had two immediate challenges. First, she was devoted to her father and had never been far away from him. Second, her new responsibility would involve extensive traveling, and she hated to travel. In the first month of her new life, her beloved father fell ill and died. She had time to journey with him and then say her painful good-bye. He told her that he wanted to give her the freedom to do God's work and that he would always be close to her even after he died. She realized that often people become more alive to us after they have physically died. We feel their closeness more now than we did when they were living. And in some mysterious and real way, they become a source of God's blessings to the ones they loved. She experienced her father close to her during all her travels, and she felt his power as she dealt with whatever problems she encountered.

After she finished her term as leader of her sisters of the Bombay Province, she was elected to the leadership team of the congregation. Now she would travel internationally and had to deal with issues that would affect the entire congregation. During her travels she was in two major accidents that have left her body in constant pain and her brain damaged. She continues to journey even with these physical and mental pains. But she reminds me that she had given God a blank check years ago, at the end of that retreat. In every dark crevice of her experiences she feels the closeness of God's presence and the warmth of God's love for her.

Thirty years later these sisters still remember their experience of that retreat, which was for me the first experience of giving the Spiritual Exercises. For each one of us it was an experience of discovering God's power through our weakness.

17 The Darkness of Addiction

The honeymoon of my ordination lasted for exactly three days; after that everyone expected me to get on with my life and ministry. After I returned from a wonderful retreat experience, I volunteered to work in one of the homes established by Mother Teresa. The sister in charge of this home directed me to one of their helpers. He had an addiction to alcohol, and she wanted me to help him. This was a totally new avenue for me, and all I had was the experience of dealing with my own weaknesses and the belief that God's power is made perfect in weakness.

This wonderful helper had lost a good job because of his addiction. His family had disowned him, and no one would marry him. I befriended him and learned that he was part of an Alcoholics Anonymous (AA) group. I continued to chat with him every time I came to the home, and we soon became friends. One day I didn't find him there and learned that he had slipped and was lying wasted in one of the bars. After a few days he returned to AA and showed up again at the home to continue his work as a helper.

We had a long and difficult talk. But what I tried to impress upon him was that who he was and what he did were two separate things. I went through several passages of the Bible to show him that he was not an alcoholic but rather the image and likeness of God, the breath of God, and a child of God—and, yes, he did have a major problem that was destroying his life. Without minimizing his alcoholism, I was trying to give him something to hold on to. He was responsible for his behavior and had to deal with the consequences of it. But he was a child of God, and no one and nothing could change that. Because he was a child of God, God loved him totally, unconditionally, just as the father loved the prodigal son and offered him a banquet. This man's behavior would never affect God's love for him. God offered to this man everything, even while he existed in the depths of his addiction. The question was, did he have the courage to receive this love?

I felt as if I had hounded this man with God's love for more than two hours. But at one point he broke down, sobbing, and surrendered to the tremendous love of God.

I knew that angels were rejoicing then. The man found his new life in the darkness caused by his addiction; he got his job back and was restored to his family. He enjoyed a happy married life until his death years later. He never went back to alcohol but found his anchor in the spiritual gifts of God. His relationship with God became more real, and this overflowed into his life and work and the people around him. He introduced me to his AA family, and we journeyed together to help many others experience what he had experienced. He died a beautiful death, believing that he was not identified by his alcoholism; he was a child of God who had fought addiction and won.

Saved by Her Son 18

After our experience with the man who struggled with alcoholism, Sister Pauline directed me to help another dedicated volunteer in the Mother Teresa home. This was a young woman severely addicted to drugs. When not under the influence, she was an effective and efficient nurse in the hospital where she worked. She had a likeable personality and got along well with people. But on drugs she became a different person.

When I first spoke to this woman she tried to flirt with me, thinking that I would be kind to her and simply accept her addiction. I made it clear that I accepted her as a person but would not support her continued self-destruction. I said to her essentially what I had said to the other person at the beginning of my journey with him, expressing that she was the image and likeness of God, the breath of God, and a beloved child of God. She was badly addicted and needed professional help. And if she sought help, our conversations would continue. She dodged her way around my clear mandate. All I could do was hang in there with her.

One day, while under the influence of heroin, she talked about her two-year-old son. Her husband was also an addict, and he became physically and emotionally abusive both to her and to her only child. Now that I knew about the child, I used every opportunity to use her concern and love for the son to move her toward freedom from drugs. We agreed that her son needed her. She admitted that she owed it to the child to give him a chance at a better life.

What eventually gave her a reason to live and get better was concern over this child, who lived in darkness while she continued in addiction. I believe that the good nurse within her came through with the wonderful qualities needed to nurture the child. And so, finally, she came to her senses and entered an effective drug treatment program. She divorced her abusive husband and raised a wonderful child. In the process she turned into the beautiful and radiant woman God had created her to be.

Today he says to this woman and each one of us: "Go now and never forget who you are: the image and likeness of God, the breath of God, and the beloved child of God."

Remembering her dark days when drugs ruled and controlled her life, she is able to live freely now in the sunshine of God's tremendous love for her. This love is not an idea but a reality of her experience. Her life is a great example of how powerfully God's love can free us. We remember the words of Jesus to the woman caught in adultery: "No one has condemned you, neither do I." Today he says to this woman and each one of us: "Go now and never forget who you are: the image and likeness of God, the breath of God, and the beloved child of God."

19 The Power of Forgiveness

Early in my years as a Jesuit priest, I found myself drawn to people with deep psychological and spiritual problems. So I decided to get a master's degree in clinical psychology. This would help me both understand and help those to whom I was ministering. My love for St. Ignatius urged me to a deeper experience of his pathway and my own growing relationship with God. My experience with human problems sent me exploring different psychological schools. But through all of this I never wanted to forget that I was only a channel through which the power and the wisdom of God could have an impact on others.

Quite a few people have told me that, without being curious or intrusive, I have an uncanny way of getting into those areas of people's lives that they have been guarding. This ability might be the fruit of my own personal search. I am constantly exploring the various canyons and crevices of my past. I find great joy in discovering and uncovering the pain of the past, finding the gifts in these experiences, and then using them to help people who have had similar experiences.

Years ago I directed a program on psychology and spirituality for a group of high school teachers. One quite eloquent and gregarious woman stood out in the group. When she stopped to talk to me after the program to say how much she had enjoyed it, I looked her in the eye and these words came out of nowhere: "You are hiding some skeletons and are protecting them with your life." At that time she didn't respond or react but simply laughed it off. But she did talk to her husband when she returned home. Then she asked to see me privately.

She had been sexually abused as a child, and she wanted her husband to know this before she spoke to me. She went on to tell me that she had been molested by a servant when she was seven years old. I suspected that something had happened even before that, and I told her so. She suddenly remembered that when she was four or five years old the neighbor's boy had molested her. When she tried to tell her mother what had happened, her mother beat her and told her never to talk about such dirty things again. When she traveled to college and back by public buses, men would walk from different parts of the bus to rub their bodies against hers. She felt numb and helpless. Even in her adult life she continued to be abused. At family and social gatherings she was the butt of jokes and thought it was because she was cute and a great sport.

With this woman, I responded much as I had with the ones having alcohol and drug problems; I stressed that she was the image and likeness of God, the breath of God, and a child of God. Only as she could believe and receive these truths was she able to claim her dignity as a person and demand the respect due a child of God. She began to appreciate herself as a reflection of God. She acknowledged all the good qualities with which God had blessed her; she could finally reverence her beautiful body as the temple of God that it was. She was able to see herself as God saw her—with total acceptance and unconditional love.

As this woman came to terms with who she really was as a child of God, she spontaneously began to forgive all those who had abused her. She believed that they had no power over her happiness and no power to hurt her anymore. Today she is still growing into the beautiful person God meant her to be.

Out of her darkness of abuse and secrecy, she has emerged an apostle, sent to others who have been victimized. Various schools and colleges have brought her to their students and faculty to tell her story and share how people can help themselves and protect themselves. She speaks to parents of kindergarten children, shares her story, and encourages them to take children seriously when they talk about being abused. She has been a means for college girls to receive the help they need, even saving some from suicide.

After she had told her husband the truth about her past, he was able to give her support and help in her healing. And so she has moved from the darkness of pain and victimhood to a renewed life as wife, mother, and effective counselor.

20 Sparks in the Darkness

My life began on a positive note and was nurtured in a warm and loving home. I knew that I was a much desired child and that I brought my parents joy. My mother would reach out in compassion to the entire world. My father was a good honest man, who worked hard his entire life.

But darkness did overshadow that childhood. Because my parents were poor, the neighbors in our Catholic ghetto could not accept them as equals. Our family was indeed poorer financially than the others, but we were gifted in other ways. Nevertheless, our neighbors found ways to despise us and keep us in our place. In short, my parents were victims of jealousy and ridicule by the more prominent leaders of our Catholic neighborhood.

Jealousy stems from the fear of not making it in this life or the next; this fear in turn generates a feeling of failure and anger toward self and others. To appreciate one's own gifts and achievements was not acceptable in our neighborhood because appreciation was often confused with pride—and good Catholics knew that pride was a sin. What motivated us was not gratitude or appreciation but fear of hell. We prayed fervently to the saints to continually intercede for us. We took up penances that would help us earn the favor of God. All kinds of devotions and ascetical practices were organized and faithfully observed.

In the month of May, the statue of Our Lady went around to each house, and Catholics of the neighborhood gathered to pray the rosary. After special family devotions on that day, the statue moved to the next house the following day. Lent was a communal practice of prayer, mortification, and penance. People would give up listening to the radio, watching TV, going to the movies, drinking, and many other activities they enjoyed. The bishops recommended reading the Bible as a good Lenten penance. They also encouraged us to make the stations of the cross and abstain from eating meat. Weekly confession was the easy way out of the sinful and imperfect life. All these practices were recommended as ways of gaining God's mercy for ourselves and the world. But rather than fostering love and freedom, many of these practices created ever more guilt, fear, and anxiety.

Oddly enough, it was because of jealousy in the Catholic ghetto and the fear and guilt fostered by those particular church practices that I began to realize my own beauty and strength. I was repelled by the neighborhood and the church, and so I focused my life in school, where I found opportunities to develop and shine. I excelled in sports, which taught me to live apart from church culture. I learned how to be a team player rather than simply compete against others. We were trained in cooperation; we played our best; and we played until the very end. Above all, we learned that winning or losing was not important; giving your best self was the only thing that really mattered. We thanked and congratulated the other teams whether we won or lost the game. We were not on a battlefield where we had to win at all cost; we were on the sports field learning to play the game of life. In school I joined the Social Service League, through which I could reach out to those less fortunate in our society. I was not focused on keeping people in their place or worried that their success might get in the way of my own. We learned that all of us are interconnected; whatever happens to one of us affects the rest of us. My parents fostered these values by their teaching and more by their example.

Every hammer stroke of negativity in the Catholic ghetto released the sparks of my inner strengths and freedom.

Every hammer stroke of negativity in the Catholic ghetto released the sparks of my inner strengths and freedom. I managed to break free of that culture so fed with fear and anxiety. I felt like an eagle that had flown the chicken coop and was now gliding high in the sky. From that vantage point I could look down at the ghetto and feel sadness for it.

The conflict and chaos of that childhood neighborhood showed up in a recurrent dream I had in those days. I would see other men in the neighborhood take my father into the corridor outside our home. While he sat peacefully on a big box of coal, they would drive a huge nail into his head. This in a way summarized my father's pattern in life: he accepted everything that came his way as God's will or God's plan. He let others run all over him and move ahead in life. At the same time, he would question his beliefs and his faith all the time. My father did not move up in the professional world, but he did grow in wisdom and grace.

The dream speaks to my life as well. I see myself sitting on that big box filled with coal—coal that has the potential to become diamonds. Coal is not as easy to ignite as wood or other fuel, but once it begins to burn it does produce strong and lasting fire and heat. Likewise, I had to work at developing my gifts and God-given talents. Once these gifts were ignited they kept burning for a long time. Each burning coal also helped light up the other coals, and once this process started it was difficult to put out the coals. These burning coals also were able to provide warmth and light to those who came close to me. Looking back at my life so far, I see that I may not always have been liked, but I was respected. I may not have had too many friends, but I was able to inspire my peers. Some of the coal in me has also turned into precious diamonds. And the process continues!

Life in the Darkness of My Religion

21

L ife had its own mysterious way of rewarding my parents' goodness. When I was twelve years old, my family moved from a very Catholic environment to a non-Christian one. In the darkness of adolescence I began to search for my own identity. I had fought hard against the identity that the Catholic ghetto was trying to dump on me, and yet I did not know where to look for my roots. In this new home we were just four Christian families among two hundred families who were mostly Hindu, with some Muslim, Zoroastrian, and even a few Jewish families. This new situation was chaotic in one sense, but it was a gift that would change the rest of my life. I had to live my traditional Catholic values in a very Hindu atmosphere. The contrast was obvious and incredible.

In our old neighborhood we had been brainwashed to believe that all our non-Catholic neighbors were living in darkness. We were the only ones who worshipped the true God, ours was the only true faith, and we would be the only ones who would make it to heaven. The priests went out of their way to drill into us that everything that the people of other religions did was inspired by the devil, and if we incorporated any of those symbols or customs in our daily lives, we would automatically go to hell. Even a simple thing like burning incense sticks in our Catholic homes was considered a Hindu religious ritual and custom.

Helped by my father's gift of questioning and my mother's compassion for the world, I began to take a closer look at my life in this new multicultural neighborhood. I found the courage to penetrate the darkness—that is, the unknown—of the non-Catholic world, and I began once again to experience wisdom and newness in my life. Thanks to my childhood experience I knew I had to make it on my own. I had to break free of a limited and distorted view of God, a fierce judge who demanded absolute commitment to his church and its teaching. I had to unloose a relationship with God that was ridden with guilt, anxiety, and fear. Not knowing what I would find, I stepped into the culture that was my heritage as an Indian, a culture that had sought

God with a relentless heart and had developed a solid spirituality for more than 5000 years.

In Hinduism I found new qualities of faith, qualities that brought health to a soul that had been damaged, not by Christianity in its pure form, but by a sectlike construction of the Christian faith. Hinduism celebrated God and life and did not scorn personal pleasure. Hindu introspection trusted that the Divine was already present deep in the human soul. And the Hindu God was personal, an intimate household God, which was a great contrast to the image of God presented by the Catholic culture of that time and place—a distant figure who was the Great Other. Perhaps most significant was that the Hindu God was not white and male.

Even as a child I realized that these characteristics of the Hindu religious experience could bring me to a healthier life of faith. And slowly I was able to open myself to the wisdom of the Eastern spiritual traditions. But I knew I had to do it alone. On the one hand I had my spiritual director who was from Spain and scrupulously conservative and on the other a church that was grounded in God's judgment and punishment. I knew deep in my heart that there had to be another way. I felt the nail of my childhood dream splitting my head and my thinking, and driving me on to new adventure.

Thus I watched my Hindu neighbors very closely. I listened to their religious stories; I looked at their lives and saw them content, open, and quite spiritual. Even though we were Christians we were always welcomed to their Hindu celebrations, and they wanted to be a part of our Christian life. Their way of praying brought me closer to a God who was personal, ever loving, and caring, a playful God who encouraged us to enjoy the legitimate pleasures of life.

Being an introvert, I spent many hours looking for a deeper and a more liberating experience of God and the answers to my soul-searching questions. I took my quest to the night skies and walked the beaches alone, pondering on the mysteries of God and the mysteries of life.

Failure and the True Self

22

Like my father, my mother was brought up in the Catholic tradition. My mother had been born in East Africa, where her father worked for the British. At age six she was shipped back to India and sent to a Catholic boarding school. While she developed her own gifts and talents, she never forgot the contradictions she observed in the sisters who ran the boarding school. In fact, many years later, when Jesuit Anthony De Mello asked her if she would join the convent, her immediate response was a strong "Never." De Mello quipped by offering to make her the mother superior. She told him that the first thing she would do as mother superior would be to close down the convent. Of course, throughout her life, my mother enjoyed wonderful friendships with nuns, but she rejected the contradictions and injustices she had personally experienced back at boarding school.

In the darkness of her early life, my mother learned that priests and nuns were no better or worse than the rest of humanity. She did not put them on pedestals and felt certain that all people were equal in the eyes of God. She never hesitated to confront priests and nuns she considered to be in the wrong; she even challenged Anthony De Mello and my Jesuit superiors from time to time. I would watch my mother in awe and admiration. She had found wisdom in the dark spaces of her life. Even when bombarded by the negative energy of those who lived quite un-Christianly, she experienced the power of her true self and practiced the loving-kindness she knew to be a divine characteristic.

My mother's wisdom in the face of negative experience reproduced itself in my life as the years went by. For instance, one year she decided that I should be an altar server. She bought a Latin prayer book, and I learned my prayers and was soon ready to serve my first mass. Now my father went to church every day, and you can imagine the joy of a father to see his son serve his first mass. This was the time of side altar masses before Vatican II. I began at first to respond my mass prayers well. Then, as I mumbled the "I confess" in Latin, I threw my head toward the priest (as I had learned), beat my breast, then threw my head away from the priest and finished my part. I waited for the priest to continue, but he remained silent for a brief moment and then yelled, "What did you say? Say that prayer again." I started all over again, but he cut me short and yelled again: "Get out! Learn your prayers and come back." I left, shamed, because my father had witnessed my being thrown out in front of the congregation.

But then my mother's gift of compassion and infinite possibilities kicked in. In the space of that dark moment I discovered the ability to flow with life without giving the negative experience power over me. I never heard my father mention this incident, but I imagine his smile of satisfaction as he watched me handle the situation. I saw another priest come out of the sacristy without an altar server, and I offered to serve his Mass. He did not care if I knew my prayers perfectly or beat my breast at the right time. From that time on I continued to serve Mass every day until I joined the Jesuits. I felt more and more confident with my prayers and my serving at the altar.

My commitment to the altar servers was a reflection of what I learned as a sportsman—I was at the altar every day in good weather and in bad. My family shifted residences, but I continued to serve Mass every day, even though I had to take the train and spend about forty minutes each way to the school. I would serve the first Mass and literally run back home, grab a quick breakfast, and make the trip back to school. I did this routine for four years until I finished high school.

In three years I was elected to lead the altar servers. As the leader, I was asked to prepare a talk and present it to the whole group. Trembling and dripping with sweat, I did give the talk. No doubt it was a mess, but I had opened my mouth, and the earth did not swallow me up. From being thrown out of the mass for not knowing my Latin prayers, I had overcome my fear of failure and of making mistakes. That messy first talk became the space in which seeds were sown for my later life as a public speaker. Imagine if I had allowed that first priest to stop my service at the altar!

Later, I wanted to join the merchant navy. This calling was by no means to meet people or see places. I was enchanted by the challenge and mystery of the high seas. It was a calling to experience the adventure of the boundless and the unknown. But I was given to understand by my spiritual director that the life of a sailor was sinful, and he steered that energy toward the priesthood. When my mother heard that I wanted to be a priest, she was very upset and said that she would never give her consent. My mother was convinced that my gifts and talents would be better utilized through another profession. She believed that I would bring greater glory to God if I went to medical school. I could reach out to those in pain with compassion and love; I could save lives. She believed that the challenge of the priesthood would never satisfy and fulfill me. The priesthood and the Jesuit life would stand in the way of the infinite possibilities that life offered me.

In contrast, my father would support us in anything we chose to do. I got him to sign my papers, and I joined the Jesuits soon after high school. Because of the love that we shared, I could make decisions contrary to my parents and still feel their enduring love for me.

Looking back at that period, I see myself as a sailor, but in the spiritual realm. I can see myself working through the adventure of the boundless and the unknown in my personal life and in my ministry. I have found the courage to go beyond sacred boundaries and seek new horizons in every aspect of my personal life. My mother's dream of saving lives through the medical profession was now being fulfilled through healing souls and enkindling the human spirit in many who came into my circle of influence.

One of the habits of soul that can most often hold us back spiritually is fear of failure.

In preparation for the Eucharist Congress in 1964, which would be held in Bombay, I joined the school choir. After about a month, the director singled me out during one of the practices. He made me sing alone and then threw me out of choir because I could not hit the notes correctly. A week later the choir director died, and my mother pleaded with the new director to take me back. I learned then to open my mouth but make sure no one heard a sound. Later, when I joined the Jesuits, I began to sing again. Before long I was singing solos and liturgies—in our chapel services but also in much larger venues. I discovered that I could indeed sing, and later I did some acting as well. So yet another time, what began as miserable failure became an experience of growth.

One of the habits of soul that can most often hold us back spiritually is fear of failure. Another unhelpful trait is our willingness to believe the negative messages people tell us about ourselves. Fear and negativity are pervasive forms of darkness, but when we undertake our life's journey with that enduring sense of possibility—the sense I observed in and learned from my dear parents, especially my mother—then we emerge truer to who we are and more capable of growing into that self, created and loved by God.

23 Healed but Not Cured

I joined the Jesuits soon after high school. My parents had never been out of India, so when I spent a year in Rome, my sister decided to bring our parents and the rest of the family for a visit. She felt that we owed it to our parents to give them a trip abroad. We visited the different shrines and sites of Rome, but my mother's heart was bent on going to two places: Lourdes and Padua.

As a pilgrim, my mother prayed the rosary, celebrated the Eucharist, and bathed in the waters of Lourdes with great devotion. On our way back to Rome she said to me, "I was not cured but experienced healing!" I have often pondered and wondered about these words. I do not know what kind of cure she was looking for, but healed she was. In the darkness of her illness, she found inner freedom through the gift of a healed spirit.

When we returned to Rome from our experience of Lourdes, my sister volunteered to take my mother to the shrine of St. Anthony of Padua. While my mother was in this shrine of her favorite saint, her whole being was transformed and she was in ecstasy. It was as if this experience made her whole life worthwhile.

My mother was named after St. Anthony. She claimed that he was her godfather and developed a close and lively relationship with him. She had such great faith in him that she could get him to find anything that was lost. I watched in amazement at how she operated and how her simple faith worked wonders. I would often sit back with the rational brain of a Jesuit and listen to her while she was on the phone. Some of our non-Christian friends would call her when they lost something precious and ask her to pray to her saint. She would innocently but with great inner confidence ask them to search a certain place in their house. If they told her that they had already searched that place carefully, she would insist that they look again. A few days later these friends would call her and tell her that they had found what they had lost at the very place she had suggested. And she had never been to any of their homes. These non-Christian friends would then ask my mother how much money they should give her St. Anthony in thanksgiving. Her response: "Find some poor person on the streets who cannot repay you and give them whatever your heart prompts you."

About a month after my family returned from a pilgrimage to Bombay, my mother experienced severe abdominal pains. At the hospital, doctors discovered that she had gallstones. Instead of taking care of the root problem, they treated the symptoms. She went from bad to worse until my family had her transferred to another hospital, where surgeons operated on her immediately. They discovered an infected pancreas; mother's condition was now critical.

My superiors called me back from Rome to India to support my family while my mother struggled to stay alive. I stepped into her hospital room and did not recognize her. The color of her body had changed drastically from bright and healthy to dull and sickly. It seemed as if she had aged overnight and had lost her young and beautiful features. Even worse, her optimistic and cheerful spirit was overshadowed by continual physical pain and listlessness.

We were not ready to lose our mother. She was one who never gave up, and nothing was impossible for her. But her physical condition grew worse. She had been born on June

13, the feast day of St. Anthony of Padua. As we sat with her in the hospital on November 13, we knew that she would either turn around and surprise us or pass on. She decided to move on to be with God and her favorite saint, Anthony.

The day my mother died, we had mass at home just for our family. During the service my father and siblings expressed to our mother one last time how wonderful she was and what a special gift she had been to each of us. She gave me the gift of infinite possibilities. We thanked God for this precious gift and then prepared to have her funeral.

It did not surprise us to see her funeral attended both by people from the streets and by others in limousines—all who had experienced a personal and special relationship with my mother. They could not believe that their young and energetic friend had died. At her funeral I preached about her beautiful virtues, loving-kindness being one of her best. I remembered how she would go out of her way to prepare a special meal for the very people in our neighborhood who had been unkind to our family. She would feed them and treat them like long-lost friends. If she had recovered from her illness, I know without a doubt that the first ones she would have invited over for a meal would have been the very doctors and nurses whose treatment had caused her condition to worsen.

In the darkness of my mother's illness and death, I was able to witness just how radiant she was. Now my dad, my siblings, and I, along with others who cherish her, have all the time in the world to take in the great love she had for each of us and to return that love by expressing it through the great gifts that she has left us her extraordinary qualities.

Lost and Found

24

My earliest memories of Dad involve the long walks he and I would take together when I was small. He never held my hand, but I walked confidently by his side. In his loving presence I always felt cared for and safe. He gave me a love for walking and taught me to take in life as it happened all around me. I noticed people, the variety of buildings, and nature. Our walks would usually end at the seaside, and in silence we would watch the waters and the ships and the seabirds. We took in the immense sky that overlooked our world. I learned to be part of the mystery and majesty of the night skies. I have continued this practice ever since.

Dad had his favorite little places where we would stop to get something to eat. While my body was being fed, Dad would nourish my soul by sharing wisdom in ways that I, as a little kid, could understand. I learned to be independent and did not need to hold someone else's hand to move along the path of my own life. He also taught me to be independent in my thinking and beliefs. My father taught mainly by raising questions. The answers were not important. He knew the answers would find us when the time was right.

At age six I was sent to the Jesuit school where my father and grandfather had both studied. For the first six months my father walked with me to school; then he left me to find my way through busy streets. Other parents would sometimes entrust their kids who were older than I to my care, to make certain they reached school safely.

But one day when I was in the third grade, classes closed early, and I decided to go to a friend's house to play. I lost track of time, and, thinking I would be late getting home, I decided to take a shortcut. I quickly got lost. I walked and walked; every street seemed familiar, but they took me farther and farther away from my home. After about an hour of walking, I began to pray. While I prayed and searched frantically for the way home, a group of street kids took my rain cap and ran away. Now I was afraid, so I cried while praying harder.

I can still remember the crowds of people walking on the streets, returning home from work. No one stopped to check on me. I thought about my home and wondered if

I would ever get back. Then a poor man carrying a basket of coal on his head (coal venders walked from house to house, selling it that way) stopped me and asked what had happened. I told him I was lost. He asked me where I lived and I said, "Princess Street," but he didn't know where that was and so took me to the streetcar terminus and spoke to a conductor. He gave me my tram fare and went away. I have forgotten the face of this Good Samaritan, but the image of his coal-covered clothes and the kindness in his voice have stayed with me forever. The sun had set by then, and my family was very worried about me. They had lit candles and prayed hard while my father and the neighbors went out in search of me. I got off the streetcar and walked home into the arms of my mother.

To this day I do not have a good sense of direction, and I get lost very easily. But I am never afraid now. I know I can connect with good samaritans who will show me the way home. Thanks to experiences of getting lost, I have seen places I would never have seen and have met the most kind and sometimes most interesting people I would otherwise never have met.

The experience of getting lost is also a good metaphor for my psychological and spiritual journey. In the interior life, I've been able to develop the same spirit of adventure, and I am not afraid of getting lost. In the dark shadows and crevices of lostness, I realize the meaning of the Chinese saying "You cannot find anything until you have lost everything." I have encountered wisdom and insights I never would have found had I remained on the straight and common path. I can be comfortable, even excited, when I lose my way, my theology, my spirituality, my God, or my very self. The darkness of being lost always opens up new and more beautiful and meaningful realms of reality. This reality becomes more simplified and more comfortable in greater darkness.

Wealth in Poverty

25

Poverty is not really a great virtue in the Eastern tradition. In fact, one of the duties in life is to earn sufficient wealth in order to pursue the goals of one's life. The poor find it very difficult to develop their personal gifts and talents and seek the higher values in life. All their energies are spent in taking care of their basic needs. At the same time, renunciation of and detachment from material things are considered great helps in attaining fullness of life at its higher levels.

One of my father's wisdom sayings was "We never had the best of things, but we never lacked anything. God always provided." I didn't realize how poor we were until years later. When I look back on those early years, I see that we were indeed poor, but as a child I never felt that we lacked anything. My father worked hard while my mother took care of the home. Any time we came home from school, my mother was there to care for us. She could make the simplest food delicious, and her presentation was fit for royalty. With all the love that my mother poured into her cooking, we grew healthy and strong. My father made sure we did well in school and that the newest little toys in the market would find their way into our home, even before richer kids in the neighborhood had them.

We could not afford to go to the movies. But I'll never forget when the first movie made in our mother tongue, Konkani, came to Bombay. My father told us that he had passed the movie theater and found out that if we sat at the bus stop outside the theater we could hear all the songs. And so we got ready the next day to sit at the bus stop and listen to the songs. But to our surprise my father had bought us movie tickets; we could not have enjoyed a treat more than we enjoyed the movie that day! My father believed that money was a means and not an end. It was meant to be spread around and spent so that his loved ones could be comfortable and happy. It is amazing how our parents stretched the little they had to make us feel equal to any of the richer kids we grew up with. I think that sometimes they envied us.

My father worked hard, and at the end of my final year in high school, he surprised us once again; he flew the entire family to our hometown in Goa. Plane journeys were very rare among the people I lived with. None of my richer companions had ever been on a plane. But my father made that possible for us. He taught us to make the most of the little we had. And he didn't wait for a special occasion to treat us—he created the special occasions. My father believed in the God of surprises, and it gave him much delight when he succeeded in surprising us and making what seemed impossible and unexpected a reality. In the darkness of poverty my father created true wealth and cultivated in us a tremendous trust in divine providence and life itself.

26 How to Live, How to Die

Our family was closely bonded, and this was our true wealth. After my mother died, my father would go every day to her grave and pray the rosary, and then sit to chat with her. He would often wonder what would happen to him after he died and would ask me if he would be united with my mother once again. Would she recognize him? When I would attempt to answer these questions, he would stop me and tell me not even to try. He was not interested in the answers I'd learned in seminary. He told me that I had not been on the other side and so would not really know.

After Mom died, my father would often sit in the house and talk with her, just as he had when she was alive. He asked me if that was crazy. I told him that Mom was still alive—not physically of course, but in a very real way. His talking with her was a wonderful way to stay close to her and deepen their relationship. After all, death is the end of a life but not of a relationship.

Then, a few years later, Dad said that one day he'd had a vision of my mother. She had entered the home and stood by the main door. She looked pretty and told him that she was very happy and wanted him to be happy, too. She smiled and went away, and my father did not see her again. He asked me what that meant. Of course, by now I had learned to say, "I don't really know," but I searched for an answer anyway. I had read about a tribe who believed that when a loved one died they stayed between earth and heaven for some time until the emotional bonds they had on this earth were lived out. Then they were free and joined the rest of the tribe in heaven and from there became the source of gifts and blessings for the rest of the tribe on earth. My father listened attentively when I shared this. My siblings were openly delighted to hear it, because we had indeed experienced special and surprising blessings we believed came through Mom who was now with God.

My father died twelve years after my mother's death. He had decided that he would die when he was eighty-six, and he did. I have childhood memories of my father's parents praying every day to die without troubling anyone.

And that is the way they and my parents died. My dad was moving around and doing all the household chores until the morning he died. But the previous day he had asked me one last question. He referred to Jesus after his resurrection, when he appeared to Mary Magdalene and the two disciples on the road to Emmaus. My father said to me that this Jesus was the same person but was transformed. "Will something like that happen to me when I die?" he asked. "I guess," I said.

The next morning he had a convulsion. My siblings got the doctor to the house, and it appeared that Dad would be all right. But he kept asking if I was coming home. I was out of town, giving a retreat, and would return later that night or the next morning. At around three in the afternoon, Dad said that he believed he would not get well. He then made the sign of the cross, looked at my siblings, and died. I rushed home only to find my father's body laid out—and yes, he had one of his characteristic mischievous smiles on his face. He had done it again, surprised us in that playful way of his. My father taught me how to live and how to die.

Chaos and Tension toward Integration

I began my life as a Jesuit with the gifts my parents had given me—namely, my father's ability to question and my mother's ability to see infinite possibilities. The spirit of the sailor also continued to be alive in me. I approached my Jesuit life as an adventure: Every obstacle became a challenge to be faced and overcome. Every horizon opened new vistas. My spirit was ablaze and unquenched, and I forged ahead in every way. From an introverted, shy athlete, I grew into a public speaker and a stage actor; I soon became a dedicated catechist, a committed social worker, and a scholar.

I lived in Bombay during the first four years of my Jesuit life. There we learned Latin and were introduced to Western thought and culture. I recognized this as preparation for a universal mission. The next four years took me to rural India, where I did the first two years of my college studies in the local language and I studied Sanskrit. I spent this time soaking in the gems of my Indian culture and a spiritual tradition that was 5000 years old. I would sit on the banks of the sacred rivers, listening to discourses about the rich insights of the ancient seers and gurus that were part of my heritage and were an integral part of my psyche. I began to have a real sense of the spiritual and the mystical.

I lived in the slums while I did my studies in philosophy and theology. I wanted to make certain that my studies were grounded in the real-life experiences of people outside the Jesuit community and outside academia. Living the simple life was challenging but did not compromise my studies.

We lived in the tension between the Western and the Eastern worlds. Some of my companions made the decision to become fully Indian. They changed their Western Christian names to Indian ones; they adopted the Indian way of life and identified themselves with the people of rural India. In the darkness of this conflict I realized that the Western and Eastern cultures are not opposed but complementary. I held on to the story of the elephant and the six blind men—each man felt a different part of the elephant and so had an accurate, yet partial description of it. Keeping in mind this metaphor, I worked to become an integrated person, one who could hold various descriptions and experiences of God in a healthy tension.

Thanks to this rich history of formation, I now possess a Western Catholic education but have learned an Eastern way of expressing Catholic beliefs. I find my life now rooted in Jesus, who was incarnated in a particular culture. Years ago I realized that I had to build my spiritual foundation on both the Eastern tradition and the spiritual heritage of Ignatius of Loyola—the Jesuit life and mission. In the apparent darkness of these cultural and mental conflicts, I found a way to live an integrated life.

28 The Transition from Xavier to Ignatius

I studied at St. Xavier's High School in Bombay, named after St. Francis Xavier. For our entire school career we learned about Xavier's life and his heroic deeds for the Christian faith. Young Jesuits were invited to the school to expound upon the greatness of this saint. For students at that school, Xavier served as both model and inspiration.

On one of the walls of the school was a painting of this saint, his face thrust forward, his hair pulled back by the wind, and the crucifix in his hand. I pictured myself imitating this saint whom I saw racing through different parts of the world with a crucifix in one hand, a bell and hosepipe in the other, baptizing anyone and everyone who crossed his path. I identified with Xavier the athlete, and, like him, I wanted to dash across the globe, winning souls for the kingdom of God. No obstacle would stop me or even slow me down.

As I cultivated mind and heart after the example of Ignatius . . . I, too, began to explore many ways to deepen my experience of and relationship to God.

But soon after I joined the Jesuits, I developed a growing attraction to St. Ignatius of Loyola, who led a small team in the founding of the Society of Jesus (the Jesuits). I was inspired by his deep spirituality and mysticism. I wanted the heart and the spirit of Ignatius to be the power that would drive the rest of my life. In a strange way, the more I knew Ignatius, the less I appreciated Xavier, that saint who seemed to be in a hurry. Xavier represented for me Ignatius at the beginning of his conversion, when he wanted to outdo all the saints in their service of God. It was during this period of his spiritual development that Ignatius was driven to do good, be zealous in penance, and become so obsessed with his sinfulness that he grew suicidal. It seemed to me that Xavier's great zeal could lead to burnout.

After spiritual friends helped Ignatius overcome temptations to kill himself, he opened up to experience a greater, more generous God who came to him in many different ways. Ignatius received mystical experiences that shaped his faith from that point onward.

For me, shifting focus from Xavier to Ignatius represented the dying of a dream I'd been building since childhood—the dream of great heroism and multiple good
works for God's kingdom. In the darkness of this transition
I began to find a more effective and fruitful way of living.
As I cultivated mind and heart after the example of Ignatius—and this cultivation is the focus of a Jesuit's early
formation—I, too, began to explore many ways to deepen
my experience of and relationship to God. While Xavier
worked to establish the kingdom of God, Ignatius was more
focused on the reign of God. Xavier was frantically baptizing people, and Ignatius was concerned about the deepen-
ing of our relationship with God.

For instance, after finishing my first two years in the
Jesuit novitiate, I began making my evening prayer in a
Hindu temple. My teenage exposure to the Eastern way of
life now found a legitimate means of expression. Encouraged by my Jesuit superiors, I introduced the Eastern way
of praying into our communities. Urged and encouraged by
Vatican II, which supported enculturation and Indianiza-
tion, my spiritual life soared. I felt that I was on my way to
becoming an Eastern mystic.

PART THREE
Darkness and the Journey of Life

Life is a mystery. And mystery involves darkness—the darkness of unknowing, of exploration, and of facing personal shadows and challenges. We cannot escape the journey; we become the people God created us to be only as we make this lifelong pilgrimage of discovery and interior growth. In this final section of the book, we explore various ways to describe this process and name what is happening to us.

Reverence: Key to the Treasures of Darkness

29

One of the key concepts that epitomizes spirituality is reverence. This word may suggest a cold and distant relationship with God and people. But reverence is a manifestation of warm affection and surging emotions that draw a person into union and communion with the Divine and with people at the deepest possible level. Unlike respect, which can exist with or without love, reverence draws a person into loving relationship and has the potential of strengthening the bond between a person and the other to whom that person shows reverence.

True reverence recognizes the sacred in all creation. The reverence that individuals experience in their relationship with God overflows into their relationships with other people, their work, and the whole of creation. When we live in the spirit of reverence, we approach every creature and every human being with love and care because we are aware that they come from God and will return to God. Reverence understands that God dwells in every part of creation; therefore, every creature is a temple.

According to poet and Jesuit Gerard Manley Hopkins, "The world is charged with the grandeur of God." Therefore, if there is one attitude necessary to continued spiritual health and growth, it is reverence—reverence that seeks union with all of life and fosters wholeness and harmony. An attitude of reverence will draw us into a nurturing and intimate union with the Divine. This intimacy in turn will affect how we experience ourselves and how we relate to all of life. Especially as we traverse the sometimes dark and shadowy realms of the spiritual journey, reverence can help us experience freedom and wholeness.

Reverence often includes the act of bowing. There is an essential connection between bowing and our ability to experience God. Bowing is one of the most effective preparations for one who wants to be open to the mystery of God and be filled and transformed by this mystery. Bowing is the outward gesture of an inner drive to empty oneself and create, in darkness and stillness, a dwelling place for the Divine. When Moses bowed before God at the burning bush, he experienced what it means to be burning and yet not consumed. He was drawn more and more into the divine life while he passed through the darkness—the trials and tribulations of his particular life on earth. When we bow before God, we, too, will slowly but surely live the divine life.

Regardless of which religious tradition we follow, we need to learn how to bow—with our bodies, minds, and spirits.

Bowing has three important aspects: physical, mental, and spiritual. To bow is to bend parts of the body in each of these three aspects. It requires a certain suppleness and flexibility so that the body does not crack or break. Genuflection, kneeling, and prostration are all included in some forms of bowing. This physical gesture of bowing the head or lowering oneself brings the mind to surrender all that it holds—namely, all the sense organs and the brain. It is ready to abandon all that has been learned intellectually. Mentally, a person bows and puts on the beginner's mind, leaving behind any sense of being an expert and opening up to many new possibilities.

Spiritually, when a person bows—lowering the face as well as the head—he or she relinquishes the ego-self. A person empties out self-centeredness and pride. We recall how God described the Israelites as a "stiff-necked people"; certainly one who is stiff-necked cannot bow. God (through Moses) tried to lead the people on their communal journey of life, but the people would not bow—not really. Bowing is an act of humility, repentance, and reverence. It purifies the mind and opens the heart to insights and mystical experiences. When we bow, as individuals or in community, gradually we realize our spiritual and divine identity.

Buddhists make the triple bow. They bow to the image of the Buddha, not as an idol but as a symbol of who this man was. It is an acknowledgement of his many spiritual and mystical experiences. Bowing to this symbol is an expression of the desire to make his experience one's own, to live life here on earth as he once did. They bow also to the *dharma,* the Buddha's teaching, to acknowledge that this pathway is now their own. And they bow to the *sangha,* the traditions and teachings of the first followers of the Buddha. Christians might find a similar attitude in the way they reverence Jesus the person, his teaching and way of life, and the example and teachings of his first disciples.

Regardless of which religious tradition we follow, we need to learn how to bow—with our bodies, minds, and spirits. Reverence clears away ego and opens us up for the divine encounter.

30 Hero's Journey and Hindu Stages

Psychologist Carl Jung gave us the "hero's journey," which is a tool for understanding personal development. It traces the interior journey through basic archetypes (models or patterns) that help us understand who we are and how we live. These archetypes are our allies. They help us to evolve, individually and communally, and reach our full potential. The hero's journey helps us grow and change into the persons God meant us to be. But every stage of the journey throws us deeper and deeper into inner darkness, where we have to work our way alone through new and unexplored terrain. If we refuse to accept this process, we will become stuck on our journey, and our lives will be limited.

An individual (that is, the "hero") begins the hero's journey as the *innocent*. A child born into this world still lives in the atmosphere of paradise, a state of grace before the Fall (Genesis 3). The child claims dominion over the whole of creation (Genesis 1) and expects all of his or her needs to be provided for. A child claims the undivided attention of every person in the environment; the goal is to remain in safe surroundings while denying that any problems exist. The *innocent*'s greatest fear is that of being abandoned, and so he or she remains very faithful to caregivers. The *innocent* can be categorized as a trustworthy and optimistic person.

But the *innocent* soon realizes the effects of the Fall. He or she begins to feel alienated, punished, and made to suffer by the very people who have loved and cared for him or her—the people who made the child feel like the center of the universe. At this stage, dominion over the whole of creation must now yield to submission to others. The person now enters the darkness of the *orphan* stage, during which he or she strives to regain the safety of paradise; or perhaps the *orphan* just waits to be rescued. The *orphan* experiences the reality of pain and suffering and fears being exploited and victimized by those more powerful. He or she will look for a religious guide who is entirely dependable, and for an all-powerful God who will rescue the *orphan* from every oppressive situation. The *orphan* learns quickly to distinguish between experiences that are life giving and those that are not. And the *orphan* gives up center stage to find connections with other people.

As the *orphan* becomes more secure in God, he or she sets out to find an identity by assuming the role of either the *warrior* or the *martyr*. The *warrior* sets out to kill the dragons and rescue others who are in distress. (The dragons as well as those needing rescuing often are not exterior people or forces but are different aspects of the *orphan*.) The *warrior* finds strength within and sets out to change the world for God or for an ideal. In contrast, the *martyr* learns to sacrifice self for others and thus pleases God and the world. The *warrior* and the *martyr* archetypes are interchangeable during this phase of development.

These first three stages, *innocent-orphan-warrior/martyr*, help us prepare for the hero's journey. The next stage is that of the *wanderer*, who is free from others and sets out to seek the deeper meaning of life and the original face of God.

The journey ends with the return of the hero as the *magician*, who aligns self with the cosmos and moves with the energy of the universe. The *magician* celebrates the experience of God in everyone and in everything. The universe becomes a home, a friendly and a welcoming place.

The *magician* finally reclaims the *innocent* as a self-actualized and enlightened being.

In the Hindu tradition, the ultimate goal of life is to experience our identity in the Divine and the interconnectedness of all of life. The process of attaining this goal isn't linear but cyclical, and happens during the four stages of life: *student, householder, forest dweller,* and *wise person.* These four stages correspond somewhat to Jungian psychology's hero's journey.

The first stage of the *student* life is similar to the Jungian stages of the *innocent* and the *orphan*. At this stage the child is weaned away from the home, where it drew the attention of everyone to itself; like the *orphan*, it becomes an anonymous part of a group. It is dependent on a teacher and has to find its identity all over again by fulfilling the duties of a student in the pursuit of knowledge. This knowledge also helps the *student* find meaning in life and prepares him or her to pursue wealth that will give it a growing freedom and a full life.

The second stage is that of the *householder*. The Jungian counterpart is the *warrior/martyr*. The person goes out to follow a profession or career and then returns to sacrifice self so that others can pursue their goals. The one who begins this stage of life as a *martyr* will then become the *warrior*. Both the *warrior* and the *martyr* have duties of loving and caring for those near and dear to them by providing wealth and affection so that all can pursue their goals.

The third stage in the Hindu tradition is that of the *forest dweller*. Today people do not leave their homes and retire into the forest to seek the deeper meaning in life. But as people retire from their professional lives, they withdraw from other mundane responsibilities and activities as well. They systematically detach themselves from wealth, including human relationships. They spend more and more time in introspection, exploring life's deeper questions. At this stage even the securities of religion give way to the spiritual quest—namely, putting our relationship with the Divine above all else. In the hero's journey this is the stage of the *wanderer*.

The stage of the *forest dweller*, or *wanderer*, prepares us and shapes us for the final stage of earthly life—that of the *wise person* or the *magician*. We began as the *innocent-orphan-warrior/martyr* or as the *student* or the *householder*. We dare to continue as the *wanderer* or the *forest dweller*. Finally, we are free to enjoy the Divine and be our true selves; we are the *wise person*, or the *magician*.

Journey of the Feminine

31

The feminine energy of humanity receives life, feels at home, and thrives in the depths of darkness. There, the feminine embraces the light and shares its life-giving energy with the rest of creation. The feminine energy is the door to our true nature.

In Chinese culture, the *yin* and *yang* represent two opposite and complementary, or connecting, principles in nature. *Yin* characterizes the feminine nature of things and is dark, cold, receptive, and downward.

Within his theory of the collective unconscious, Carl Jung called the feminine energy *anima,* which is the Latin word for "soul." According to mystic Meister Eckhart, the ground of the soul is dark. In fact, the essence of life is dark. And so the soul of a person, male or female, is the feminine energy and is most often encountered in some form of darkness.

Jesuit theologian Karl Rahner said emphatically that the future Christian is either a mystic or nothing at all.

Jesuit theologian Karl Rahner, SJ, said emphatically that the future Christian is either a mystic or nothing at all. What Rahner said about a Christian, I believe, applies to people all over the world today. There is an unprecedented thirst for the spiritual and the mystical among different cultures and people. Mysticism belongs to what Jung called feminine energy; this energy is intuitive, which means it goes beyond the mind and the five senses. In her article "Structural Forms of the Feminine Psyche," (1951; 1956), Toni Wolff, Jung's closest associate, described the feminine journey insightfully as divisible into segments characterized by the predominance of one of the four archetypes: the *mother*, the *warrior*, the *lover*, and the *magician* (or *mystic*). According to Wolff, these four basic structures can be seen in every woman. As the woman matures she will integrate a structure and move to the next until she reaches the mystical, or magical, state. What Wolff sees in a woman, I believe, can be applied to any person who is evolving to his or her fullest potential. Every individual possesses feminine energy and will pass through the basic feminine archetypical structure to become a fully evolved person.

The first stage of feminine evolution is the *mother*. A person's life begins with a nurturing relationship with his or her mother. This relationship is the foundation of all future relationships with people, with the Divine, and with life itself. In a very real way, mothers are the cornerstone in the future lives of their children. During the dark times of growing up, it is the mother's love and more especially her hope and confidence that help the child grow into a healthy and happy adulthood and old age.

The mother is not the sole female influence in the life of the child. Grandmothers, aunts, godmothers, and women neighbors and friends are often willing and able to lay foundations of love and compassion for self and the rest of the world. The downside is that they have the power to make or break the self-esteem of a child. It is interesting to note that a mother's influence does not end with childhood but runs through the person's entire life. Long after mothers are dead, their voices still influence their children.

Having established this foundational *mother* relationship, we now move on to the second stage of the feminine journey. This stage is characterized by the *warrior*, who is the powerhouse of energy. Loyalty and honor are two distinguishing qualities as the *warrior* pursues the purpose of life. Personal comfort and safety fall by the wayside, and death is a plaything while the *warrior* is on the battlefield of war, spirituality, or morality. The *warrior* does not hesitate to destroy that which is negative and harmful to the world and always finds creative ways of dealing with obstacles. The *warrior* is a doer and totally detached from life, having an infinite capacity to withstand psychological and physical pain in the pursuit of the goal.

At this stage, we move out of ourselves to help the world very actively and to rescue those in distress. We now want to express the love relationship in reaching out to fight against unjust structures and take care of those who are in need. "Whatever you do to the least of my brothers and sisters you do unto me" now becomes our motto.

The *warriors* who are anxious to rush out into the world must first turn inward. This inward battle takes them deep into their own darkness. They then begin to preserve and protect the *mother*-relationship. They are motivated not by fear of punishment but by gratitude for all they have received. In the *warrior* stage, sin is not what they do but rather a breach in the relationship with the Divine.

When the relationship between the *mother* and the *warrior* is reconciled, then the effects overflow into the way life is lived out.

Having mended and deepened the *mother*-relationship, the *warrior* now passes on to the journey's stage characterized by the *lover*. This is similar to the return of the prodigal son, the person who has the courage to celebrate with the one he has offended. The *lover* will accept both strengths and weaknesses in self and others. The *lover* is now at home and settled in all relationships.

The *lover* has all five senses highly developed and takes in life as fully as possible. The *lover* is a worshipper of all things beautiful, both inner and outer. Finally, a *lover* wants to stay connected with every person and all of life. A *lover* does not recognize limitations, always going beyond sacred boundaries to seek new horizons.

The *lover* then quite naturally becomes the *magician* or the *mystic*, who lives the fullness of life in inner peace and freedom. The *magician* feels like a drop in the ocean and the ocean in that drop. *Magicians* are finely attuned to life's energy and have the ability to make that energy come alive in people under their influence. The *magician* is a sage and the knower of secrets. The *magician* has the capacity to detach from the chaotic situations of the world and stay anchored in the essential truths and resources that exist deep within. In fact, it is the *magician* who keeps all the other archetypes energized, humane, and in touch with the ultimate purpose of life.

The Feminine Face
of God

God made humans according to the divine image and likeness. Humans, in turn, throughout history, have created God to fulfill their personal and social needs. Many of our creations have been anthropomorphic; others we thought of as cosmic forces or philosophical principles. Regardless, often our perceptions and images of the Divine have been male, female, or some combination of the two.

Often our perceptions and images of the Divine have been male, female, or some combination of the two.

The dark feminine sacred principle dominated the earliest religious conceptions of the world. Archaeologists have discovered that female representations of the sacred existed more than 30,000 years ago, from India to western Europe. From the earliest written records and material artifacts, we find that feminine attributes were attached to the sacred in the religious outlook of all the original centers of Western civilization: Mesopotamia, Egypt, and Crete.

The mystery and wonder of the birth-giving female made the goddess reign supreme. This goddess was connected with the life-giving principle: fertility, growth, and life both in this world and after death. Once the male role in fertility was discovered, the cult of a young male god, the son-lover of the goddess, was introduced. Later, a more egalitarian couple replaced this image. Only at a much later stage do we find a pantheon dominated by male gods or a religion devoted to a single male deity. While the sequence of histories was not so direct, there was a general development over time away from feminine symbolism of a sacred presence and toward male imagery.

The historical and social processes that resulted in more male-centered images and concepts of the sacred are not clearly understood. One possibility is that an agricultural society and more intensive urbanization fostered male dominance, both socially and in religious conceptions. Also, the growing cult of a male sacred principle was linked to the triumph of invading seminomadic, less civilized, warlike, and highly patriarchal populations who worshipped the male deity either as head of the pantheon or as the sole deity.

In religions having a female deity, the goddess creates by pouring her life into creation. Humans are invited to intimacy and joyful participation in life. Basic life processes, especially birth and sexuality, are affirmed. The female imagery is involved in a broad range of cultural activities and socially valued goals. We don't know if goddess worship reflected feminine dominance in society. We don't know if female deities allowed women more independence, respect, and power than did societies that worshipped primarily male deities.

We do know that most religions today are male dominated and designate women to standings below men; in some cases, women are clearly oppressed by these patriarchal systems. This is why so many people—teachers, spiritual directors, and scholars—have tried to rediscover the feminine faces of God. Some religions and cultures do a better job than others do of bringing together the masculine and feminine.

In Indian mythology, the *ardhanarishwar,* which literally means "half woman" or the feminine energy, is considered to be the soul of the universe. This goddess is often portrayed as the supreme creator who split her body into half man and half woman, thereby balancing her own feminine qualities with the masculine ones. The masculine forms of gods need the feminine *shakti,* or power, that will make them more effective. The same holds true for the entire universe—the external masculine form is set into motion and kept alive by the internal feminine energy. This mythology reflects the Western saying that behind every great man there is a great woman. This woman has often been kept the in the dark background of the man. If she can manifest her power through the little cracks in the man, then the man begins to shine brilliantly before the rest of the world. This feminine power and inspiration is often recognized years after the woman has died.

In the *Samkhya* school of Hindu philosophy, *prakriti* and *purusha* are the feminine and the masculine embodiments of the universe, and they manifest the power and presence of the Divine. One way of understanding this reality is to look at *prakriti* as the feminine creative energy that will make the masculine power of *purusha* effective. *Purusha* creates the elements, while *prakriti* is their life force. *Prakriti,* the feminine energy, is the eternal energy, while *purusha,* the masculine energy, is always creating forms that come and go. *Prakriti* creates the intellect, while *purusha* creates the mind and the five senses. The mind and the senses keep the *purusha* entrapped in the material world; it can liberate itself when it discovers the *prakriti,* which is the only true and lasting reality.

My best insights into the Buddhist tradition came out of encounters with people in the Buddhist parts of India, Sri Lanka, Hong Kong, Singapore, and the Philippines. I led retreats, and retreatants would share with me their responses to prayer experiences. The responses of the men were quite different from responses I found in other cultures. These responses were filled with compassion rather than judgment; they were charged with intuitive imagination rather than intellectual ideas; they focused on personal life experience rather than on intellectual statements. The lives of retreatants were based more on spirituality than on dogmatic religious teachings; furthermore, they quite naturally related religious beliefs to their personal lives.

I became curious about what was at the bottom of this approach to spirituality, which was new for me to encounter as a spiritual director. I concluded that the Buddhist foundations of the cultures had much to do with the people's responses in prayer. Even though they were baptized into the Christian faith, their faith expressions came from the Buddhist collective unconscious. The Buddhist tradition is founded on compassion and equanimity, and their symbol is the lotus. The lotus grows in dirt and rises above the surface to bloom as a stately flower, spreading its fragrance as it basks in the sunlight. At night the flower closes and sinks underwater only to rise and open again at dawn, untouched by the dirt. This pattern of growth signifies the progress of the soul from the bondage of the material world, through the waters of experience, and into the bright sunshine of enlightenment.

Compassion is manifested most effectively by the feminine *bodhisattva* ("enlightened being") Kwan Yin, whose Sanskrit name means "born of the lotus." Her Chinese title signifies one who always observes or pays attention to sounds and so is attentive to our prayers. She embodies the attributes of total acceptance and unconditional love and is accessible to everyone. Devotion to this goddess of compassion involves no set ritual or dogma but inspires us to cultivate within ourselves those particular refined qualities that all beings are said to naturally possess in some vestigial form: compassion, love, service.

Kwan Yin evolved from her male prototype, Avalokiteshvara, "the merciful Lord of ultimate enlightenment." According to one of the myths about Kwan Yin, she was a Buddhist who through her ideal life on earth had earned the right to experience the ecstasies of nirvana, eternal bliss. Like Avalokiteshvara, while standing in contemplation before the gates of paradise, she heard the cries of suffering humanity. Her compassionate heart prompted her to make a vow that she would not pass on to her eternal bliss, but live in the heart of humanity until all other beings had experienced inner freedom. Kwan Yin is the embodiment of compassionate loving-kindness and thus enjoys a strong resonance with Mary the mother of Jesus.

33 Mary: God's Feminine Face in Christianity

Today the feminine dimensions of the sacred are getting more and more attention, even in Judaism and Christianity. Much of the energy involved in this renewal of Christian symbols undoubtedly is motivated by secular and liberation ideologies. There is a growing awareness that in the Christianity introduced in the colonial world, Jesus was born and died but never lived or rose from the dead. The whole of Christian living was centered on Christmas and Lent, climaxing with Good Friday. For the needs of day-to-day living, people turned to their various devotions to Mary. The energy that Christians drew from Mary became real and effective in the dark world that was subdued by the ruling classes in the name of God and religion.

Theologians are working to give Mary her rightful place by falling back on Scripture and tradition in the church. Mary the mother of Jesus is that feminine principle that permeated Christian life from the very beginning. Christian theology is based on God's revelation and self-communication through Jesus Christ. Mary is God's channel through which we experience Emmanuel, God with us. Not only did Mary give Emmanuel human birth, but by the same act she was also drawn to share in the divine work of salvation through her personal union with God—thanks to her total surrender to God.

The early literature of the church fathers compares Mary with Eve. While Eve represents humanity in a state requiring salvation, Mary stands for redeemed humanity and becomes the channel of salvation for the world. Eve lived with Adam in ignorance and without consciousness, but when she invited Adam to eat the fruit of knowledge and consciousness, Adam called her the mother of all the living and the source of life. Mary becomes this new Eve, the model of full knowledge and consciousness.

Mary's way of living is reflected in her response when God invited her to become the mother of Emmanuel: "Let it be done to me according to God's word." This is easily translated as "Let life happen to me according to God's word." When good things happen, Mary is there, taking in the hosannas without clinging to the good times. When they shout "Crucify him," she is fully present, taking in the pain without clinging to the pain or resisting it. As she lives through the darkness of pain or joy, she is purified and enlightened. She ponders the mystery of life in her heart and fully lives her life.

Mary receives God to take birth in her, and then she is driven to share this knowledge.

Mary teaches us to live the fullness of life as God's favored one, God's image and likeness—the breath of God. Mary's cousin Elizabeth offered insight into the secret of Mary's way of living when she exclaimed, "And blessed are you because you believed what the angel said." Mary's response to Elizabeth teaches us to find our true identity and make the most powerful feminine prayer: "All generations will call me blessed."

Mary receives God to take birth in her, and then she is driven to share this knowledge. She rushes to her cousin Elizabeth. Elizabeth, who had known the darkness of being without child, has experienced the hand of God within when she became pregnant in her old age. She therefore is now disposed to understand and receive that same divine love that has blessed Mary. When Mary arrives, the babe in Elizabeth's womb leaps for joy. This is such a profound lesson for those who want to reach out to people in need and want to transform the world. Unless we receive the Divine in our hearts, no one will leap and jump for joy. We can be eloquent in our words and brilliant in our writings, but without our receptivity to God, no one's heart is touched and no lives are changed. Also, a true experience of God is for the edification of others and overflows into reaching out to others.

The mystery of Jesus' birth offers us a practical lesson in freedom from all things that humans fear: poverty, contempt, and humility. As we identify with Emmanuel, we, like Mary, realize our divinity. Along with Mary, we find a common bond with the simple shepherds and with the wise ones, the Magi.

In John's Gospel, Mary finds her identity with the Logos. In calling Mary "woman" (John 2:4), John identifies Mary with the woman foretold in Genesis 3:15, who stands with the Logos to crush the head of the serpent. This is the same "woman" Jesus gives us from the cross (John 19:25–27) to be our mother and our model; she shows us how to work out our salvation by finding our divine identity in God and experiencing how we are connected to the whole world.

Life's Deeper Mysteries: A Conversation

34

I once met a group of women who were thinking seriously about what would happen to them after they died. I was surprised at their concerns and worries because they were so different from the women I encountered in the Gospels and in other parts of the world. These were committed Christian women who, having raised their families, were now semiretired. They were economically quite comfortable and now used their time to read and reflect on the Bible. They had just finished reading Matthew's Gospel and concluded that they had not done enough good works to merit heaven. And so they had come up with a list of things they could do to collect merit so that when they died and appeared before God, their good works would earn them easy entry into heaven. They were going to look for poor people they could help, volunteer their time in hospitals and nursing homes, and keep looking for other opportunities to do good works.

These were women, but I realized that their approach to heaven did not come out of true feminine energy. The spiritual feminine does not keep accounts, just as no mother keeps account of all the things she has done for her children; a mother just loves. Any person, male or female, who loves out of the feminine energy of the soul, loves without keeping an account or looking for a reward. Although these women were very loving and caring, the good works they sought to do were not loving acts. They were looking to use people to gain personal merit in heaven. It reminded me of a social worker who once said that she wished there would always be poor people so that she could help them. What will happen to these kinds of people who, because of age or illness, cannot help others but need others to help them?

What this group of women got from Matthew's Gospel was that you had to do plenty of good works or else there would be bad consequences. The bad deeds would be punished, and so these women were concerned about others who appeared to be living sinful lives—they would be in real trouble come judgment day. They were thinking specifically about people who spend time in the casinos in Las

Vegas, and were concerned that they would all go to hell when they died. They had to change and repent. And these women decided to pray for their conversion and for the salvation of their souls.

While these women were talking about Matthew's Gospel, I suggested that there is so much more in Matthew's Gospel than judgment. For instance, Jesus says, "When I was hungry you gave me to eat; when I was thirsty you gave me to drink." These women would be confidently shaking their heads, remembering all the good works they had done, all the donations they sent to various charities, and the many people they had helped and prayed for. I thought about how surprised these well-meaning people would be to hear the Lord say, "I am not talking about you. I'm talking about those who say, 'Lord when did this happen? When were you hungry, when were you in need, when did I feed you?'" You see, that is the true response of the feminine soul; it does not keep a record of the good it does. The attitude of a person overflowing with energy of the feminine soul is: What's so special? What's so great about this? Why do I deserve a reward?

I continued my conversation with these women, taking them to the passage in Matthew where Jesus compares the kingdom of God to a priceless pearl or a treasure hidden in a field. The pearl is formed in the darkness of the oyster, and the treasure is hidden in the darkness of the earth. When the person finds the pearl or the treasure, she sells everything she has just to have that priceless gift. Those who find the treasure in spiritual darkness identify the absolute in their lives, and nothing else matters; they give up everything for that absolute.

As we reflected on this dynamic, we realized that what really counts is not what we do, or give, or give up. What really counts is this: Have we found the treasure? Do we have the pearl? Have we found our identity in the Divine? Is God's total acceptance and unconditional love for us a reality we feel from the inside out? This treasure cannot be earned but is given freely to anyone who knows how to receive it.

On the Last Day, God is not going to ask us to give an account of how much we sold in order to buy that pearl or how much we gave up for it. God will look for the pearl that was formed in darkness. Do we have the treasure that was hidden in the darkness of our life experience?

[The Magi] were ready to risk everything, to get lost, to be fooled, to make mistakes.

I drew these women to the story of the Magi, who came from the East and followed the star that led to the Christ child. The Magi were searching for the deeper mysteries of life and were ready to give up everything for the star that attracted them; they had spotted the treasure and the pearl. Their quest did not seem rational nor was it logical; they were just following the star. They were ready to risk everything, to get lost, to be fooled, to make mistakes. Like the Magi, once we follow that star, we will find the mystery, the mystical, the Divine, Emmanuel, God with us. But like the Magi, we will have to plough through the darkness of the night and the depth and darkness of our own lives.

When we started our conversation with Matthew's Gospel, these women were obsessed by the reality of their particular judgment and the final judgment. They were going to be prepared for the Last Day when the human race will be gathered before God, and it will be either eternal reward in heaven or eternal punishment in hell. One of the women asked me if I ever think about what will happen to me after I die. I said, "Yes, sometimes. But I am not afraid because I have such confidence in God that no matter what I do, no matter what happens, I know that my God will draw me in and take me to the divine Self." I added that if God is not a God of love and the father of the prodigal son, then I preferred to be in hell. I am confident that when I die I will be with God. This intuition does not necessarily have the reason and logic of solid scientific proof or theological certainty. I cannot tell you how I know this. I just know. I cannot justify this and give you reasons that will convince you without a doubt. I just know. This ability to know what is unknowable—it is a gift of the feminine divine in each one of us.

Old Age, Fear, and Love

35

One of my favorite ministries is to the elderly, and one of my themes for the elderly is that God is waiting for us to show up so that God can show off. That is my firm belief. I cannot tell you how many elderly people I have accompanied to their deaths, who died happily awaiting God's presence and celebration.

I would sometimes tease these folks by challenging them about the sins they confessed. I once asked an elderly man if the sins he confessed when he was younger were the same sins he was confessing in his old age. He said, "Well, most of them." And I chided him, saying, "Of course, the more interesting ones are the sins of youth, so now you are left with the boring sins. And you think God would be interested in those?" God does not care about the stupid little things we do. I wonder, too, if God cares even about the great good that we do. God is simply waiting for us to show up!

Another elderly gentleman said that he was getting ready to die and had not done enough to gain heaven. He had, in fact, spent many years working to bring people closer to God. He would leave holy cards at their workstations, and his conversations were always about believing in Jesus and making him their personal savior. He did a lot of charitable work. But now that he was old and feeble and could not leave his home, he could not do all those good works, and that bothered him.

Then and there, I told him to stop loving God. He looked at me in confusion, and I think he was about to ask me to leave. But I told him that for the rest of his life he should give God a chance to love *him*. I suspected that his zeal to love God had often come in the way of his receiving all the love God had for him. I said that the only love we can give to others and to God is the love that we have allowed ourselves to receive. This man had spent all his life trying to do good to gain merit in heaven. I told him that he was like the older brother in Jesus' parable of the prodigal son who said, "For so many years I have *slaved* for you and never disobeyed any one of your commandments." But when his father responded by saying, "*Everything* I have is yours," the son did not know how to receive it—he was too busy *slaving* at doing good and collecting merit.

In fact, [the prodigal son's] love for life may have been what led him out into the world to get lost and make a mess of his life.

Past a certain time of life—especially when we have reached old age—it's pointless to try to love God more through the good works we have been building on since earlier decades. Eventually we feel that we haven't done enough and that we can't do more of the same. So, how about a change? Let's spend the rest of life allowing God to love us. God will probably be greatly relieved when we stop trying so hard and simply open up to love.

The prodigal son in the story knew how to enjoy life and receive the gifts and blessings of his father. In fact, his love for life may have been what led him out into the world to get lost and make a mess of his life. But he took the risk, he got lost—and he came home, knowing that his father was a fair, merciful, loving man.

Are you afraid of dying? Do you think about the afterlife? Are you still concerned about that judgment? Where did we get these images of the afterlife that inspire so much fear and guilt? Who passed them down to us? When the Buddha was asked about the afterlife, he wanted to know if this was a philosophical question or if the questioner really wanted to know. If the person really wanted to know, the Buddha would say that the death could be arranged, so then the person really would know for sure about the afterlife. Short of dying early, we can allow ourselves to celebrate the gift of life.

Creation and Sin: Two Views Make the Whole

36

We can see the masculine and the feminine energy in the two creation stories of Christianity. In the first account, a distant God creates everything; there is order in this creation, and humans are the pinnacle of it. This account of creation seems to have a liturgical resonance. During the first three days, God separates the light from the darkness, the waters from the sky, and the waters from the dry land. During the next three days, God decorates what is separated. God places the sun in the daytime and the moon and the stars in the night, the fish in the sea, and animals and vegetation on the dry land. On the sixth day, God creates man and woman and gives them dominion over the whole of creation, ordering them to increase and multiply and subdue the earth. This is a masculine way of life—to have dominion over all creation and to subdue the earth.

The masculine God creates the Sabbath, and on the Sabbath you come—where? Not to God—you come to the temple. And who is in the temple? The priest is in the temple, and the priest takes your offering to God. And if you have a special offering once a year, the high priest will enter the holy of holies with your offering. So you cannot relate directly with God but need intermediaries. That is the masculine experience of God whereby the male is in charge of your life and your relationship with God. That is a masculine way of relating with God: to have dominion over creation, and on the Sabbath to come pay your dues.

In the second chapter of Genesis, this God who was out there, now comes down and is playing in the clay. This God has a name, Yahweh, and has a personal relationship with the whole of creation. Yahweh-God is willing to get dirty in order to turn the clay into the shape of a man and breathe into that man divine life. This act is feminine. A mother does the same when she brings a baby into this world. When you breathe your life into another life, you become a part of that life. God then creates woman, not from the feet of the man so that he can trample upon her, and not from his head so that the woman can dominate him. God creates woman from the side of man so that they can be equal partners and companions.

This personal Yahweh-God does not give man and woman dominion over the whole of creation or call them to multiply and subdue the earth; this more feminine God wants the man and woman to till the earth. This God wants them to become part of God's creative energy and continue God's creative work. God has given us this world not to dominate and subdue it but to re-create it and to fashion it into what is beautiful and divine.

It is even more interesting in this account that God first creates man. If this man were left alone, there would be problems—it would be a world completely defined by the male. So God takes a rib out of the man and makes woman as a companion; therefore, feminine energy can balance masculine energy in the world.

In the first chapter of Genesis, God creates male and female at the same time. He makes them in the divine image and likeness. And so in each of us there is both male and female, masculine and feminine. Male and female can be seen as two different persons in Genesis, but you can also see that in each of us there is maleness and femaleness, there is feminine energy and masculine energy; it takes both to tell the story fully.

We also have masculine and feminine approaches to the downfall of humanity. In the masculine way of looking at the Fall of Adam and Eve, God forbids the man and woman to eat the forbidden fruit from the tree of knowledge; if they do, they will die. This God wanted absolute control of knowledge. Adam and Eve disobeyed God and were banished from Paradise. In fact, God placed cherubim with fiery swords to guard the tree of life so that humans could never again get near it.

Because of original sin, human life would be forever altered. Humans would be afflicted by guilt, fear, and anxiety, and their lives would be ridden with pain, trials, and difficulties. The masculine energy focuses upon original sin that is passed down to every person in the human race. The only way out for the human race is to have Jesus come into this world and make retribution for the sins of Adam and Eve. Jesus had to die on the cross to redeem us from sin and its consequences. It is through the death of Jesus that the gates of heaven will be opened again, and it is through a person's baptism in Jesus that the original sin is removed. It is through Jesus alone that humans will find a way back to paradise. Anyone who does not follow this path will be condemned and will never enter the kingdom of God.

The feminine energy looks at the same mystery of the incarnation quite differently. In the text of Genesis 3 there is no mention of sin or Satan. Jesus would therefore be born into this world for the glorification of God's creation—the re-creation, the completion of creation—not for humans alone but for the whole of creation. The feminine soul looks at Adam and Eve and sees in their story not pride or disobedience but a state of ignorance without consciousness. It was the serpent that drew them to knowledge and consciousness through the feminine quality of intuition. The original text of Genesis introduces the serpent as the creature God had made and having secret wisdom that no other creature possessed. Until the fifth century, the serpent was never equated with Satan but was a symbol of wisdom, mystery, and healing. The serpent has feminine energy and therefore approaches the woman with the invitation to eat of the tree of knowledge; if she ate the forbidden fruit, it would make her wise, opening her eyes, and she would see herself just as God had made her, in God's own image and likeness. With feminine intuition, the woman believed the serpent, ate the fruit, and offered it to her husband, who also ate. Then their eyes were opened, and they realized that they were naked.

Nakedness is a beautiful symbol of transparency; now they could see themselves as they truly were, "like" God—that is, in the image and likeness of God. The woman had told the serpent that if they ate this fruit or even touched it, they would die. Now they eat the fruit and they do not die; on the contrary, Adam will call his wife Eve, because she is the mother of all the living. In fact, she becomes the source of life. By eating the forbidden fruit, Eve and Adam gain intuitive knowledge and consciousness of who they really are.

Jesus therefore comes into this world to give us full consciousness and full knowledge of who we are and what life is all about. Jesus comes to give us life, life in all its fullness (John 10:10). Jesus comes into the world not to redeem us from our sins but to reconcile us to God and to one another.

Jesus comes into this world to teach us how to get rid of our skins, which were put on in the Garden of Eden—skins that made us different as men and women, saint and sinner, priests and nuns, and laity. Those skins create a hierarchy in society and religion; they separate Indians from Americans from Chinese from Russians. Jesus' mission is to help us see ourselves in our nakedness. In the transparency of ourselves we will see the image and likeness of God and realize the divine breath that is present in all of creation and every human being. We recognize the interconnectedness of life.

Why did Jesus die on the cross? Because of what he preached and the life that he lived; there is no greater love than this, that a man lay down his life for his friends. And what did Jesus preach? Faith that is expressed in a living relationship with the Divine. Tax collectors, prostitutes, and sinners believed Jesus and were therefore rushing into heaven before those who held power and were certain of their rightness.

So we see that even in our sacred stories—the Creation and the Fall—there is a process of becoming. There are risks we must take and dangers we must face. We must break free, become naked, and even leave paradise in order to experience God.

37 Being Set Apart

Before we were born, we were set apart and sent into the world with a divine message. If we do not witness to this message, no one else will. This message expresses the meaning of our lives and is shared through our personal gifts. Sometimes the more unique our gifts, the more alone we feel. In the darkness of being set apart, some become afraid and either deny their gifts or compromise themselves in order to fit in and not be so lonely.

But the realization and acceptance of being set apart refines our self-image and brings forth freedom, courage, and a new zest for life. When a person allows his or her life to be unique, that is the beginning of an authentic life—the life God means for us to enjoy.

Some people believe that recognizing their own talents is a sin against humility. They aren't confident in expressing their gifts, and so they bury their talents. But when they realize that they are capable of thinking independently—that they are truly set apart—then everything changes. They develop the longing to do things in a meaningful way even though it might differ from how other people operate. They begin to see infinite possibilities in helping others, especially by passing on to them the deeper longing to be themselves.

All the wonderful qualities that make a person unique can be overshadowed by the fear of rejection.

All the wonderful qualities that make a person unique can be overshadowed by the fear of rejection. This fear keeps people from expressing their opinions, ideas, needs, and feelings. Fear of rejection clouds their vision of the Divine within them. Such fear can actually cause us to push away from the Divine, which only increases the loneliness.

Here is a firsthand account of a religious sister who was praying about what it means to be set apart.

When I reflect on my past, I realize that I was trying to fit into the groups of women around me; I was trying to adapt to their ways of being, to their likes and dislikes. In my friendships and other relationships, because of the fear of rejection and fear of losing the other, I was trying to pay attention to others' expectations, likes, dislikes, and comforts. I sacrificed my own wants and desires and martyred myself for the others. In my work and mission too, because of the fear of being different, I was trying to push aside all the exciting possibilities that came my way and the many inspirations I was given. The more I did this, the more I became alienated from my true self. As a result, I increasingly suffered from loneliness and dissatisfaction. It is with this pain of loneliness that I began my retreat.

Three fourths of the first day, I literally felt as though I was groping in the darkness; I couldn't understand what was happening to me. This went on until I met with my retreat director. He brought to my notice how insightful I was about the negative patterns in my life. He told me that I was good at reflecting on these patterns and coming up with effective ways of dealing with them. But he noted also that I refused to do the same with the positive parts of my life, especially with the gifts that God had given me. My director pointed out that I was set apart with very special gifts, and he challenged me to look at them and accept them. He asked me to pray over Galatians 1:15–20, in which St. Paul shared his belief that God had set him apart from eternity to preach the good news to the Gentiles. This would set him apart from the other apostles, who worked with the Jewish community. The Gentiles were culturally, socially, and religiously alienated from the Jewish community. But St. Paul also believed that he was blessed with the necessary graces to live out his personal mission.

As I was reflecting on this text, I suddenly felt divine grace rush into me. In a fraction of a minute I understood that each person is set apart for a purpose from eternity, and our existence on earth is meant to fulfill that purpose. I saw clearly how I was escaping from my true self with all the gifts and special graces given to me. I assumed the uncertainty of what it meant to be set apart. I was drawn further into the darkness—darkness created by my fear of being alone and apart from others. Once I reconciled myself to the mystery of this darkness, it seemed as if a treasure chest burst open and I received the courage to take responsibility for being myself.

I now understand deeply that embracing this darkness will bring to fullness the special gifts God has given to me: the capacity to think independently, the longing to do things in a meaningful way though it might differ from others' paths, the ability to see infinite possibilities in helping others both materially and psychologically, and a deeper longing to be myself.

38 What the Darkness Brings

I recall being loved, accepted, and appreciated during my childhood years. As the firstborn, I was greatly anticipated by my parents, and they showered on me their love and dreams. As I grew older, I enjoyed friends and companions, who also accepted and valued me.

Yet, in the midst of these positive experiences, a sudden loneliness would surprise me. My mind would latch onto thoughts of death and dying, though not in an obsessive, suicidal way. In fact, with those thoughts I would experience a sense of the freedom that death would bring. That progression of thoughts recurred over a long period of time. I didn't quite understand what was happening. Also, I grew irritated with myself. I kept thinking, *Why can't I just enjoy the goodness of life instead of making myself miserable?* In addition to these thoughts, I often became over-sensitive to what people said and to life in general.

Then I began to understand that whenever I experienced feelings of jealousy, sadness, anger, or anything else that provoked a negative response, I would also experience a deep yearning—the desire for my true self. As negative responses would draw me into the tunnel of darkness, and as I made efforts to face them, the desire to be free from the negativity would also well up. What I came to understand, eventually, was that my recurrent meditations about death were manifestations of an unconscious longing to die to the false self.

When we push away the darkness—of loneliness or irritation or anything negative—we are passing up a profound opportunity. When we allow ourselves to experience the negativity, that very negativity will stimulate our deeper longings for wholeness and freedom. Then we can learn to treat difficult situations simply as part of life; then we can look beyond others' behavior and accept them as they are. Also, we can accept ourselves as we are and where we are, and our negative experiences—both inner and outer—as important aspects of our development.

39 Hating Father and Mother

Unless you hate your father, mother, brothers, and sisters, and your very self you cannot be my disciple.

—Jesus of Nazareth

These words seem quite harsh, especially coming from the mouth of Jesus. But there is wisdom here. We need to take a good look at our lives and ask ourselves: Is my life an imitation of someone else, or is it my true, authentic life? Do others have a remote control to our responses, or are we compelled on the journey by our own convictions?

Little children reflect the image and likeness of God and in a real way have dominion over the whole of creation. They live life most spontaneously and in total freedom. But no sooner do children begin to speak, they are taught words, values, and behaviors that are colored by a definite family tradition and culture. The process of distorting the divine image and likeness begins in the family. The voices of our parents—especially the voice of mother or whoever was primary caregiver—sink deeply into our subconscious and unconscious and set the course of our life.

For many of us, religious training begins in early childhood. Whatever our tradition, it conditions us to specific expectations, fears, beliefs, and values. And so another layer of voices is added to that of our parents. Later, we go off to school, and the process continues. If we are fortunate, the school years provide some space in which our gifts can bloom. At the same time, the values of the prevailing society are reinforced. Knowledge is dumped into us, knowledge we are expected to integrate and pass on. Sometimes the very process of learning what is expected will kill our earliest and truest beliefs. And another powerful dynamic is going on—our social interactions with peers and teachers. We feel the compulsion to fit into a group; we may well compromise ourselves just to meet the approval of our peers. This pattern will continue in some form as we leave school and make our way in the world—in our workplaces and community involvements. Some of us are forever sacrificing our true selves to keep the peace in our families and our social groups.

There is never a time along this precarious journey of becoming when we should not stop and ask ourselves, Is this me, or is it someone else?

So when Jesus talked about hating mother, father, sister, and brother, I believe he understood very well how easy it is to relinquish our own God-given power to learn, grow, and act according to our true nature. There is never a time along this precarious journey of becoming when we should not stop and ask ourselves, Is this me, or is it someone else?

When we work through—and sometimes against—the light that those in authority have shed over our primeval darkness, we will find that authentic self in silence and aloneness. In this state we do not have the security of traditions and structures, of elders and teachers. We have only the self and God. And from this darkness we can truly say, "It is no longer I who live but the Divine who lives in me!"

Spiritual Repose: Culmination of the Spiritual Journey

The spiritual life is about the interior journey toward the Divine. The destination of the journey is a state in which our desire and love for God overshadow everything else.

This journey often begins in the mind. We want to know and understand the mysteries of the spiritual life and of life itself. We are hungry for books and articles and read as much as we can; we attend seminars, workshops, and retreats. We make copious notes and try to reflect on the gems that we pick up from this search. We go through ecstatic moments when we find words and phrases that touch us deeply or that express what we always knew or experienced. We receive revelations that help us understand the deeper meaning of life. We make resolutions to live a better and richer life. Such experiences often manifest in visible physical and emotional signs. Tears, change of body temperature, and even loss of speech are manifestations of the beginning of a long inward journey toward God, who dwells in the darkness that is our very core of existence.

As we persevere on this road and go farther on the spiritual journey, we find that our heart, as well as our mind, has become engaged. Our mental reflections begin to translate into experiences of the heart. We experience divine bliss and a sense of unity with God but are still conscious of our individual selves in this divine union. Words become inadequate to express an inner transformation. We begin to find security—not in outer structures but within ourselves. We begin to place our hope in God alone. This hope is grounded in our ever-increasing faith in God. This faith slowly moves from a mental acclamation of creeds and dogmas to a personal relationship with the Divine. The effects of this relationship now overflow in loving service to all who come into our world.

The momentum of this relationship now takes us into the deep recesses of our being, where we will encounter darkness and aloneness. At this depth, there is no consciousness of the mind or the heart or even the body. It is an experience of total presence, awareness, and pure consciousness. Oneness with the soul is then attained in a most loving way, and all the cells of the physical body are flooded with divine love. Our life energy begins to flow more freely in us and slowly takes over the whole of us. We can be in this state for hours, days, weeks—until we shift the awareness from the soul back to the physical body. After a long period of this way of being, we will live our physical life in a soulful way. This is the only stable unchanging reality; all else is ever changing and does not bring everlasting peace or happiness.

Our spiritual journey finally climaxes in tranquility: all that we experience is peace and quiet—spiritual repose. It is here that we begin to experience God as God truly is. During this stage we will pass beyond any sensible visions of God. The Father, Son, and Holy Spirit flow into One. This union with the divine essence springs forth from the very depth of our being and permeates every aspect of our life. It is a gradual commingling with the Divine until it is no longer we who live but the Divine who radiates in us and through us to the world around us. Every moment of our lives is part of the eternal time; every place we are in connects us with the rest of the universe. We begin to feel that we are fully connected with the whole of creation.

Growth that happens in the darkness allows us to be drawn deeper and deeper into the Divine.

So when it comes to our spiritual journey, growth is not necessarily happiness or good deeds or even holy living. Growth that happens in the darkness allows us to be drawn deeper and deeper into the Divine. This dynamic so consumes us that the very energy of God overflows from us as individuals, spilling into everyday experience and transforming the whole world into a sacred place.

Also by Paul Coutinho, SJ

AN IGNATIAN PATHWAY
$14.95 • PB • 3309-8

A collection of more than 100
excerpts taken from the Spiritual
Exercises, the Autobiography
of St. Ignatius Loyola, and his
Spiritual Journal. Each entry is
followed by a short meditation
written by Coutinho that amplifies
the easily overlooked mystical
dimension of Ignatian spirituality.

HOW BIG IS YOUR GOD?
$12.95 • PB • 3294-7

Coutinho challenges us to grow
stronger and deeper in our faith
and in our relationship with God.
To help us on our way, Coutinho
introduces us to people in various
world religions who have shaped
his spiritual life and made possible
his deep, personal relationship
with God.

Also by Paul Coutinho, SJ

JUST AS YOU ARE
$18.95 • HC • 2721-9

**Available in paperback
November 2012!**
$12.95 • PB • 3761-4

In *Just as You Are*, Coutinho, SJ,
helps us move forward in the
confidence that God's love is
unconditional and that God
simply asks us to embrace
that unconditional love and live in
it on a daily basis. A native of India, Coutinho combines Eastern
sensibilities with Ignatian principles and practices to show us
how to stop spinning our spiritual hamster wheel—futilely
acting as though we can somehow earn God's love and favor—
and instead move forward in the unfathomable love of God
already present in our lives.